Carl-Auer

Invisible Dynamics

Klaus P. Horn/Regine Brick

Systemic Constellations in Organisations and in Business

Translated by Colleen Beaumont

2005

Published by Carl-Auer-Systeme Verlag: **www.carl-auer.com**
Please order our catalogue:

Carl-Auer-Systeme Verlag
Häusserstr. 14
69115 Heidelberg
Germany

Cover: WSP Design, Heidelberg
Printed by Koninklijke Wöhrmann B. V., Zutphen
Printed in The Netherlands

ISBN 13: 978-3-89670-491-7
ISBN 10: 3-89670-491-5

Title of the original edition:
„Das verborgene Netzwerk der Macht"
© 2001 Gabal Verlag GmbH, Offenbach

Bibliographic information published by Die Deutschen Bibliothek
Die Deutsche Bibliothek lists this publication
in the Deutsche Nationalbibliografie; detailed bibliographic
data is available in the Internet at http://dnb.ddb.de.

Contents

· · · · · · · · · · ·
Foreword

By Otto Wassermann

The constellation methods described in this book have been used successfully in our company for years.

As specialists in process-orientated management for over fifteen years, we have organised procedures and supply chains in business and industry using our own simulation software. Using this software, we can simulate the procedure and handling of future contracts and materials. We create a situation as though the planning, procurement and production were actually taking place.

Identify bottlenecks using simulations.

The simulation identifies potential bottlenecks so that they can be corrected before they can cause delays or missed deadlines or affect productivity. With problem areas cleared, contracted work and materials flow freely through the company and supply chains.

An ingenious idea, but so simple and unusual that it often meets with scepticism or even complete rejection. *"Simulation isn't the same as reality!" "Do you actually think you can depict our complex procedures using software?" "There's no way it can work."*

Communications up-date

These are some of the reactions, plus a lot of head shaking, that we are often confronted with when we approach new customers. For many years Dr Horn and his team have helped us to deal with this reaction constructively, using systemically orientated training. Instead of retaliating with a defensive, "Yes, but ...," on our side, we have been able to recognise the signs of interest embedded in such negative reactions. The ice is soon broken and, after a while, our customers themselves can't remember why they were previously so blind to something as easy and effective as this. In the process, they are also learning to overcome barriers and anxiety and to work together as a goal-orientated team. Our trainers call that a "communications up-date", one that alters old patterns and habits that are no longer useful.

Nonetheless, like many of our customers, I had a similar reaction when Dr Horn told me one day that using a different kind of simulation he could depict a human business system and smooth out problem areas just as we were doing with technical business systems. I felt that it was clearly impossible, because you would have to deal with people in all their complexity. Of course, he interpreted this as a sign of interest on my part, and so it led to our people sitting down together to get acquainted with this new kind of simulation.

We presented Dr Horn with a customer situation that we felt was a complete muddle, one that had already cost us many sleepless nights, and we challenged him to demonstrate how he could put it in order.

Confusing situations made clear

Using representatives, we set up a constellation of the system, and we were truly amazed. It was crystal clear to everyone exactly what was going on. This confusing muddle was suddenly laid open like a book. Every person in our group felt as though a veil had been dropped, we could see where the problem lay and what the solution was. The real surprise, however, was still to come when, less than three months later, the exact solution that had appeared in the constellation actually emerged in reality!

Why constellations function, we still don't really understand, and neither do the systemic experts, but the fact that they do and that they lead to solutions, can be documented.

These days, to the benefit of our customers, we work successfully with Dr Horn and his partner as specialists for business systems: we at the technical level, and they at the level of human interaction.

To get the most benefit from this book, regard your own objections as signs of interest. You will be richly rewarded by valuable, stimulating input that perhaps may sometimes seem like magic.

Otto Wassermann
Chairman of the Board, Wassermann AG

Introduction

Do you understand the significance of a good team line-up in football? Do you know how important network connections are for the marketing success of a company? If you do, then you are already familiar with some of the most important principles of this book.

Well-connected

Today, a business is considered well positioned and "well-connected" when it is in a strong market position, with executives skilled in human resource management. Behind the rhetoric lies more than just a passing trend. It reflects the importance of the "network connections" within the organisation for the success or failure of the operations. Because awareness of these connections is at an unconscious level, it has been little used up to now, denying us a valuable navigational tool. The network constellations, in which our business ventures are embedded, are by no means accidental. These interpersonal systems, which we know as teams, departments, companies, and markets, follow certain laws, and their success depends on the degree to which they conform to these laws.

The systemic constellation method offers a tool that can depict complex interconnections and reciprocal effects in a clear and simple way. In widespread networks as well as clearly defined teams, this method also helps to sort out entanglements and to recognise hidden resources in obstacles.

More inner democracy

As in any new development however, this method also presents you with an unreasonable demand. What is it? It demands that you risk more "inner democracy". To profit from this method, you have to dethrone your rational mind as the sovereign ruler in ways of learning, problem solving and innovation. Relinquishing this out-dated

9

monopoly on the transfer of information and energy makes much in the business world more attractive and colourful. Letting go of the monopoly of a linear-analytic method also opens new pathways in business management and consulting. It complements the potential of logical thinking and digital analysis with the invisible knowledge and concealed information already existing in the organisation's system.

In systems of human interaction, there exists a kind of invisible field of information, similar to the way the Internet contains a vast wealth of information about concrete questions. The information we scan on the web can only be used when we make selections and, similarly, the information contained in an organisational system can only be accessed through a particular procedure. Contrary to current trends, the selection process in a system of human interaction requires an analogue procedure, the language of symbolic images.

To decipher them, we need a special kind of high performance processor – the emotional intelligence of the right brain. The concentrated information about a business system is stored in unconscious images that can be made visible through the elegantly simple process of the constellation method. These images have an enormous advantage in that they are comprehensible to everyone. Complex situations and problems that would be exceedingly difficult and time-consuming to work out using logic and analysis become clear at the speed of a mouse click.

Culture of the organisation

The product here can be neither counted nor increased. It is however what determines the success of a business and its ability to adapt to the future. Current nomenclature refers to human capital and the culture of an organisation. Why has the culture of an organisation become a central topic of discussion? It is the glue that holds the entire complex structure together. A sense of belonging and loyalty of the members to the organisation are important components of this glue. Under stress, it becomes clear whether the glue will hold, or whether the support structure will collapse.

When the culture of an organisation binds and supports, it is most clearly visible at the interface between organisation and individual. This is where the track is laid that determines whether the train will proceed to its destination or be diverted to a siding. The enormous significance of the "switching" factors has become clear only now in our age of information. Thomas Sattelberger, member of the Lufthansa regional board, described human capital as "the real bottleneck in business".

The future belongs to networks, both global and regional.

The success of a business is dependent on how harmoniously the organisation's system works and what place it finds in the complex market networks; and it depends on whether those running the business understand and respect the laws of human systems.

The "human capital" of a company consists of not only the right employees, but also the right bosses! Those in decision-making positions have to attend to systemic balance if they want to achieve a stable balance. This is true for small family businesses just as it is true for multinational concerns.

Systemic constellations and coaching:
A new approach to problem solving ...

The procedures presented here provide access to the information in the network of a company. Therefore, systemic constellations and systemic coaching may emerge as *the* problem solving method of the future. This is a new approach that is spreading throughout the world from its origins in Germany, and initial scientific research has confirmed the positive effects of the method in a variety of well-known businesses.

... for organisational systems in business and industry

Although the constellation methods are increasingly attracting attention in the public eye, there has been a paucity of material available to those wishing to apply the method in businesses. With this book, we hope to communicate the usefulness of this new approach in business. The book is meant for practical application, and you will gain from the examples presented here, whether they have to do with strategic business decisions, team development or personal goals.

Regardless of your position in your organisation, the application of systemic principles can give you insight into problems, help you in making critical decisions and open new perspectives for the development of the organisation.

For over twenty years as trainers and consultants, we have worked with the questions, problems, goals and visions of our cus-

11

tomers, who include individuals as well as businesses of all sizes and in various fields. The innovative method of systemic constellations, which is what this book is about, has become an important tool in our repertoire of skills. With the help of this method, we have been able to help many customers to find solutions to complex situations, to clarify goals and to develop new perspectives. Solutions can often be found in situations where the tools of classical training and coaching would not have been sufficient. Nothing is as successful as a method whose time has come! Nonetheless, other, complementary approaches are sometimes needed, particularly in implementing solutions in everyday situations. We have included an effective approach for moving from macro-systems to micro-systems, a transfer which can be critical to success.

Overview of the book

What can you expect in the following chapters? In the first chapter we look at the invisible mechanisms that influence a business. Chapter two details the development of the systemic constellations method and describes what actually happens. Examples of constellations done with our customers allow you a glimpse into the practice. These constellations are documented in the third chapter. In our seminars and lectures, we are often confronted with interesting questions about systemic work. As you may be asking some of the same questions, a selection of many of these questions and our answers have been included in Chapter four. Because individuals must apply the solutions that emerge, the interface of the macro-system (the business or organisation) and the micro-system (individuals) is of paramount importance. Our approach to systemic macro-micro-coaching can be found in the fifth chapter. The conclusion in Chapter six contains a checklist with which you can begin to apply systemic principles in your company or organisation immediately.

1. The Organisation's System – Your Most Important Working Capital

1.1 THE INVISIBLE CONTROL SYSTEM IN YOUR BUSINESS

The whole is more than the sum of its parts.

It would be a mistake to believe that you, as a businessperson, run your business alone. As manager or employee, if you are of the opinion that your boss or the board of directors are setting the priorities, you are overlooking something critical. In actual fact, *everyone together* is running the organisation. This is not meant in the sense of "we're all in the same boat", nor is it in the sense of the common ownership of the Soviet era.

It is not only those belonging to the organisation who participate in the success or failure; others also play a role – for example, the customers, the share holders, the users, the competitors and perhaps foreign affiliates. Like a network, they create a powerful whole that is more than the sum of its parts.

The whole functions as a *living system*, whose dynamics have effects that are often in direct opposition to the decisions made by the company executives.

How is this possible? When we consider individuals, it is very clear that everyone has their own blind spots and from time to time acts and reacts unconsciously. At the very least since Sigmund Freud, it has been generally accepted that the unconscious has a powerful influence on our actions, feelings and thinking. Our rational thoughts and actions have even been compared to a floating nutshell, and the unconscious the sea. As long as the sea is calm, the nutshell captain believes he is in control.

A company also has an unconscious.

It is not only individuals that are influenced by the unconscious, but also human systems – families, organisations and businesses. Martin Buber pointed to this conclusion with his well-known statement that the unconscious is not *in*, but rather *between* individuals. This unconscious *between* people is not only a phenomenon of mass psychology, as observable at a football match, pop concert or campaign speech. Even more, it is a powerful but invisible structure in organisations, departments and teams, that functions according to its own rules and principles. Therefore, we speak of a "system" and systemic rules.

Within the system, we are all connected to one another.

What is a system?

What is a "system", actually? Simply stated, a system is a number of elements that are connected to one another in continuously changing relationships. With any change in one element there is a simultaneous change in all the other elements. This is not true of all technical systems, but it is true of all living systems, including people, organisations and businesses.

If everything in a company system is in a constantly changing relationship, it means we have to let go of the comfortable habit of thinking in terms of cause and effect.

Within the networks of living systems, there is not always a cause first and then the effects. Effects may show up for which we can find no cause at all.

An effect may be a result of a cause that has arisen simultaneously and invisibly in a different place and is itself an effect stemming from yet another cause. From the good old cause-and-effect chain, we come to a circular image in which the events emerge in various places simultaneously and lead to results, also in various places.

Simultaneous and reciprocal effects in systems

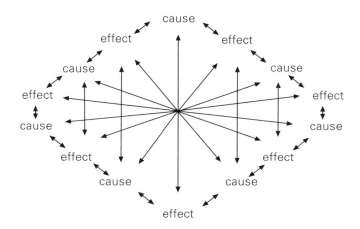

Assigning guilt achieves nothing.

One response to difficulties, which is still widely popular, is to look for the guilty or responsible person. This falls short because it doesn't solve the problem. Seen systemically, the "guilty party" may not be a causal factor, but may be functioning as a symptom carrier for the system. In such a case, this person's culpable behaviour could be the effect of an invisible systemic connection. Firing the "guilty" person would be a solution something like, *"If the red warning light comes on while driving, remove the light bulb and drive on."*

The organisational consultant Grochowiak looked at systemic reciprocal effects using the example of a frog pond:

Let's imagine a pond and look at the population density of the frogs occupying this space. The population will grow precisely in relation to the amount of food available. If the number of frogs increases in response to a surplus of food available, there will be less food available, which leads to a decrease in the frog population. With fewer frogs around, the quantity of available food increases, which allows for a responding increase in the number of frogs, and the cycle begins anew. (Grochowiak, Castella a. Klein).

15

The obvious is the most difficult to see.

It remains to be said that frogs suffer from another problem that we humans may also share; they do not always recognise their food! A frog can only identify a fly and catch it if the fly moves. If it remains motionless, even right next to the frog, it is invisible to the frog. Therefore, a frog might starve to death, surrounded by the most luscious flies, if they are lazy enough to lie still. We would do well to learn from the frog example, and not overlook solutions that are sitting right in front of our noses. It is well known, however, that seeing what is obvious is particularly difficult!

Systemic pictures instead of analytical descriptions ...

To solve complex systemic problems, business leaders and consultants have to change their habitual avenues of awareness, and free themselves from linear-causal descriptions and explanations. This is where the constellation method can complement classical approaches to consultation by portraying the organisation systemically rather than analytically.

Using this method, you can easily get an overview of the situation as it is at the moment. Tensions that are preventing progress become visible immediately, for example, difficulties between production and marketing or between management and a foreign affiliate. You can see whether the position of a department or individual is right in the larger company context, and how things need to be changed to improve the functioning of the whole.

... makes solutions clear.

When systemic connections become clear to our customers, many react with, *"It couldn't possibly be that simple! We have invested so much time and money over the years without ever really solving the problem!"* The pain of such recognition is well known in many contexts. These days, for example, simple, inexpensive software solutions can solve problems in logistics that used to involve a major investment of time and effort, often with unsatisfactory results. Force of habit, however, can keep companies from accepting such solutions, sometimes for years. Often, the resistance is not due to economic or technical considerations. Now and again, even the most innovative managers appear to get caught in a strange reluctance to accept something new.

How does it happen that people who have proven themselves many times over with their daring and good business sense, are suddenly plagued by doubt? They are responding to a "gut" reaction, an instinct based on the impact of a shift in the systemic whole. No matter how smoothly innovative software simplifies a technical procedure, the effects at the interactive, human, systemic level can be disastrous. To avoid this kind of turbulence, any major restructuring steps should be accompanied by a systemic check. Proponents of a new technology or streamlined process may feel discouraged by a half-hearted response to this newly introduced improvement. Because they are looking at the linear, analytical aspects of the situation, they miss the systemic level, which is critical to success.

The systemic level is critical to success.

Of course it is important to optimise a company technologically, but the match is being played elsewhere. Even in the age of information technology, businesses are *human* constructions and they function as all interactive human systems – simply, logically, and consistently – like a biological organism. Our bodies, too, are complex organic systems that require a particular kind of nourishment, a certain amount of movement, and a set quantity of fluid. They react with irritation to the poisons of our civilised life, particularly when combined with stress. As we know, those who are aware of the systemic laws of the body and act accordingly have an easier time than those who consider themselves impervious to these demands. Interactive systems behave in a similar way. Here, too, we have a choice; we can make an effort to understand and conform to the rules and demands, or we can wilfully ignore them in favour of short-term gains and suffer the consequences later.

Human systems function according to the powerful, unconscious laws.

Also in the organism of a company, the system, there is an underlying awareness of what is useful and what is harmful. This awareness does not belong to any individual and is not based on expert analysis. More accurately, it exists in a kind of informational field. What this informing field is, exactly, and how it functions has not yet been fully investigated, but we can benefit from its effects nonetheless. Just as in IT, even if you don't understand what the Internet is and

17

how it functions, you can still use it if someone explains what you have to do to select what you need. Then, you can call up a wealth of information at any time from any place.

Using systemic constellations, you can tap into the informing field of your business. You can select what you need from this network that receives all relevant information about the web of relationships in the company.

How does such a field of information work in practice? It works *unconsciously*. Because the systemic information is not consciously employed by the individuals involved, but remains inactive, it is usually interpreted as a "hunch" or a "gut" feeling. For example, the head of production in a company may not know exactly what is going on between sales and a customer, even though it affects him directly.

Let's say that the sales department has promised an important customer a large delivery within four weeks, even though the production schedule shows that it will take two months. This agreement takes place without the head of production knowing about it, but he "knows" something nonetheless. An uneasy feeling creeps in when he looks at his production schedule and he decides to talk to the head of sales about the projections for the quarter. This is already a sore point between the two, since the production manager continually feels over-ridden by the sales manager and keeps trying to defend himself against the consequences of his colleague's hasty decisions.

When information from the system is inactive, only vague feelings are available.

In this situation, the production manager is not mistaken in his "gut" feeling. He discovers that the sales manager has once again disregarded his instructions. The salesperson, on the other hand, is insulted that, instead of appreciation for a top sales contract, he gets grumbles and complaints. Sparks fly between the two, not for the first time. The conflict becomes a continual state of tension that makes clear communication and a good solution difficult. Using a modern approach in good clearing sessions, the two managers have still not made any progress. This is where the constellation method could be of help to bring the systemic dynamics to light, resolve the conflict and ease the tension in the field for the future. In a constellation, the systemic information is consciously activated. In the second chapter you will see how the method functions.

What practical use is there in making the informational field conscious in a company?

Just as a glimpse into the unconscious may free people of suffering, the recognition of systemic barriers in a company can support the emergence of new solutions. Buried resources are freed up and cooperative work is facilitated.

When systemic principles that allow a business to function smoothly are not followed, problems arise. If you were to fill a Formula 1 car with diesel fuel, even the best driver, in the optimal pole position, would still have no chance of winning. This is a consequence of ignoring technical rules, not a lack of skill.

Systemic laws are simple and sensible.

In both the laws of nature and the laws of systems, ignorance of the law is no defence against consequences, just as breaking the law in our society has consequences, whether you are aware of the law or not. Now, we all know what kind of petrol our car needs, but we often tank up our body, a biological high-performance machine, with diesel instead of super. As we commit our little sins against our bodies, we are, of course, fully aware of the combined effect of cholesterol, stress, and too little exercise. Knowing is clearly not enough to make us act in a way that leads towards what we want. Therefore, we have to learn through insight or suffering. If insight does not produce results, a confrontation with acute consequences will make us stop and look for a different solution.

1.2 CONSCIENCE AS A SYSTEMIC COMPASS

There is a special force that directs individuals as well as organisations either towards their goals or into diversions – conscience. In this context, it has little to do with moral principles or noble ideals. It is, rather, a kind of compass that tells us if we are on the right course. Our systemic conscience provides us with a sort of social orientation, not in the moral sense of informing us what is good and what is evil, but rather if we are going in the right direction in our environment.*

---

* See also the works of Bert Hellinger for more about how systemic conscience functions.

Systemic conscience gives directional orientation,
not moral judgement.

This precise inner compass points to the north factually, without reference to morals. In business systems, the correct direction –"north"– may differ radically. In a traditional German small family business, as an orientation for everyone in the system, "north", might indicate punctuality, precision and a readiness to put in an effort for the sake of the company. Values such as punctuality and exactness, or expectations of voluntary, unpaid overtime provide the how and what in a system like this. *"What do we want to achieve? To deliver precisely made products, on time, to our customers. How do we want to achieve that? Through maximal individual effort and involvement."*

Whether an extreme effort and involvement is effective and whether it will bring economic rewards, is open to question, but that is not the issue here. "Effectiveness" is not a value that determines "north" in this company. There is no doubt that all the people in this company, from the youngest trainee to the top boss, are all brought into line in a systemic way. Everyone in this system has a good conscience if he or she works evenings and weekends willingly, and a bad conscience about a leisurely coffee break. This is not particularly unusual, since the orientation described here is widely accepted in our society and therefore embedded in a larger systemic network.

The amoral (not *im*moral) nature of the systemic conscience becomes clear when we look at the example of a Mafia system, in contrast to the example described above. There is not one iota of difference in the way the conscience operates. A member of this criminal organisation has a completely clear conscience, for example, when he demands protection money from a restaurant owner in his territory. The "what" and the "how" lie directly "north" in his system. Along with his share of the money, he might get a clap on the shoulder from his colleagues or boss as a sign that, *"You've done well. You belong to us."*

Belonging, at all costs

Belonging to a group means survival. This inheritance is ours from our origins in the animal kingdom; the various stages of evolution stored in our behavioural repertoire. For our closest relatives, the mammals, belonging to the pack or the herd is a matter of life or death. The lost sheep is as doomed as the rejected lion cub.

Because we are equipped with the strongest possible motivation to assure our place in our current social system, it is extremely difficult to change counter-productive behaviour that shows up in the larger organisation.

For example, when high-precision, quality production is in opposition to the demand for speed and price reduction, there is a problem. What good are perfect, high quality products if no one will buy them because the customer can achieve his own goals with cheaper electronics delivered faster? It would appear to be time to change the basic orientation! However, the workers and bosses run up against their systemic conscience.

Example: Mechanical engineering

The crisis in German mechanical engineering in the last decades shows us that a change in orientation is exactly what does not happen, even when total ruin is the inevitable consequence. The members of an inter-personal system would rather pay that price than go against their systemic conscience. This stance, in the case of mechanical engineering, in Germany has been strengthened by the arrogant belief, formed in the successful years before, that good German quality work could never be replaced by electronics, and certainly not by products from Asia. If a systemic simulation using constellations had been done at the beginning of this crisis, it would have been clear what the effects would be of the attitude of German industry towards electronic innovation and towards Asian competition. A clear picture of the future consequences would have made corrective measures possible.

1.3 THE INVISIBLE LINES OF POWER

System laws work invisibly.

Who or what determines your business strategies? Economic calculations alone could hardly be responsible. In the last decade we have experienced a boom of "soft" factors. Corporate identity, company philosophy and development of a vision are all buzzwords. An import from the USA is the current trend to identify human resources as the actual bottleneck in business. However you define your goals and strategies, your business does not operate only according to its self-declared tasks and goals. It is also determined by invisible laws, which operate most powerfully for the good and for the bad.

21

Because these laws are hidden, people in an organisation are usually not aware of them. How do you feel their effects? Well, how do you notice that you have overstepped the biological laws of your own body, perhaps on New Year's Eve? A hangover gives the feedback the next morning! When you respect the biological limits and laws, you feel good in your own body. In the same way, as a member of an interpersonal system, you feel supported and strengthened when you observe its rules, and you feel personally weakened when you ignore them.

Typical symptoms in a business that indicate that the laws of the system have been violated are: employees and customers suddenly leaving, internal power struggles, sabotage, massive drop in sales or crippling stagnation.

Without systemic support, financial reorganisation rests on a weak foundation.

These alarm bells have usually been misinterpreted up to now. What do executives do when things slow down and get stuck, when market share and sales drop and employee turnover increases? They call for restructuring and financial reorganisation! The effectiveness of these steps is questionable, as some "stars" of restructuring have publicly demonstrated. Firstly, not all problems can be solved through control. Secondly, in ignorance of systemic effects in the situation, financial reorganisers may make things worse, despite the best of intentions. The system reacts as if to an invasion and mobilises the last resources available and uses them counter-productively. It functions similarly to a human immune system, which responds to an attack by producing warning symptoms.

Human systems – families, companies, and organisations – strive to survive, so they protect their members from attack from without. If one of the systemic principles is seriously disturbed, an unconscious rebalancing occurs, with uncontrollable effects. What gives rise to this phenomenon?

A company functions in a network of people, information and technology and is closely connected to other networks, such as customers, markets, and so on. Every move has an effect on all those involved. Therefore, there is an unspoken awareness in the network of what is good, what disturbs, and what will weaken or strengthen the whole. When parts of the network are working against one another, or pull out of the whole, the system will function poorly. A problem often arises at this point, like a warning of an overdrawn account.

In the practical work with companies, departments, teams, and organisations, certain principles keep appearing, the "laws" according to which the system functions. Regardless of the size or kind of organisation, consultants and researchers have observed how people in such systems react with the certainty of sleepwalkers to respect or disregard for these principles. They experience their work surroundings as harmonious when the laws are observed and react with confusion when the principles are violated. In the next section we will present an overview of some of the important laws and principles of systems with examples and explanations of their basic function.

Principles favourable to systems

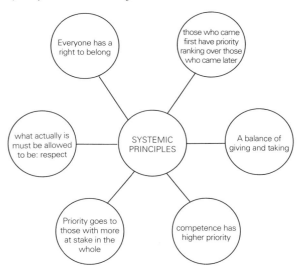

What is, must be allowed to be: the principle of respect

Acknowledging reality opens prospects for solutions.

What does it mean that what is, must be allowed to be? First of all what this means is:

Reality cannot be denied. To be capable of action, all the members of the system have to recognise and have respect for the way things actually are.

23

As simple as that sounds, it is unfortunately not so easy in practice. All too often critical developments in an organisation are glossed over. It happens again and again that company leaders themselves cannot admit a downward trend. As a result, they cover up the true situation from their colleagues and workers. Everyone feels, however, that something is not right. In some cases, the extent of the crisis is known quite precisely throughout the company, but no one utters it aloud.

Meanwhile, the denial peaks in a collective fantasy. *"A major job is about to come in that will turn the company around."* In families there is a similar denial, for example, when everyone knows that the father is terminally ill, but they hide this fact from each other. When denial can be set aside and reality faced, the collective acknowledgement of the actual facts of the situation has a freeing effect and opens the system to solutions. Those involved look with courage squarely at the naked reality in its entire, often painful enormity. Only then are they capable of decisive action.

There is another form of acknowledgment that is perhaps familiar to you from everyday work life: *active recognition of the givens.* In situations where there is uneasiness or worry about expectations or tasks, it can clarify things to bring up the basic systemic reality. Rationally, it doesn't make much sense to say something that the others already know. Nonetheless, it has a powerful effect when something is said, such as, *"You are the boss of this department and I'm your employee." "You are the customer and your satisfaction is paramount for me." "You have been in the company for 12 years and I'm new here."* In this way, the speaker communicates that he or she is aware of both of their places in the system and acknowledges and confirms that.

The balance of giving and taking

A "grace period" for new employees

Have you ever come across one of those teams, in which a few team members do the lion's share of the work? The unevenness of such arrangements is clear to an outside observer, but is typically not clear to the team participants. Sometimes those who are carried by others are new, inexperienced team members, who still need some time to work themselves into the position. Compensation is easy and often occurs naturally if the newcomer spontaneously acknowledges what they have received. They might express this by helping out wherever they can, even when some of the work is not in their job description. When long-time colleagues, however, lean back and take it easy while others do all the work, they are freeloading.

Success in a team is only possible when such imbalances are corrected. When balance has been restored, a new challenge arises. Are those who have been carrying the load up to now willing to distribute the work more fairly? This cannot be taken for granted. In order to do this, they must be willing to hold themselves back and to accept help from others. For capable people, that demands a degree of trust that may be more difficult than doing everything themselves.

It is not always more blessed to give than to receive.

You may have seen situations where a dangerous imbalance develops because the team leader refuses to accept the support and help of team members and denies others the chance to develop. Instead, a boss like this is always there for the team, helps without being asked, takes over difficult tasks and even solves their problems for them. The flip side of such a willingness to help is that real teamwork cannot develop. It is difficult to bridge the gap between the leader's competence and the team members' dependence. When the team members have no opportunity to perform well themselves, they soon feel useless and either leave the company or quit inside themselves. The saying that "it is more blessed to give than to receive" may be true in a religious context or in the boxing ring, but systemically, it leads down the wrong path.

Balance is essential for successful mergers.

How does a balance of giving and taking function in larger contexts? Does this also have meaning in multinational concerns? Look at the current trend towards mega-mergers with their eye on the shareholders. If a company executive is looking only at the shareholder value, he or she is perhaps ignoring the efforts of the workers who should be thanked for the success. Their achievement is taken for granted, without acknowledgement or appropriate compensation. Such imbalances harbour the potential for one of our greatest dangers, when small firms or poor countries are left empty-handed following mergers and globalisation. Of course, great ships do not sink immediately from listing to one side. They initially appear to steam on ahead on a course to success with no damage – until the crisis suddenly breaks out and becomes apparent.

The right to belong

You belong to many different social systems. You belong to your family of origin (your parents and siblings), to your present family (your spouse and children), and to one, or perhaps more, work systems. Have you ever considered how it would be if someone challenged your right to belong to your own family or your own business? Unfortunately, this is something that is happening more and more. In restructuring and mergers, the right to belong is chronically disregarded. Following the changes in the companies and in the names, often no one in the new structure has any idea who founded the company all those years ago. Or, the founder is deliberately no longer mentioned.

No statute of limitations on the right to belong

There is, however, no statute of limitations on the right to belong. The founding father still belongs as much as the current executive. The same is true of employees who have retired or who have been let go during lean times. It strengthens the company when they are remembered with good will. Just as the founders, these workers were once the company, and they form the roots of the present firm. Practically, it has proven useful to hang photos of the founders of the firm in appropriate places in the company to honour their position. Do you know of such rooms or foyers, where you can admire busts of the founders, scenes from the company's history, old products or machines? The positive effect of such a conscious remembrance is clear because employees and visitors like to stop and have a look. You can feel that the roots of today's success are seen and honoured here.

Problems due to injustice

Everyone who belongs to a system, must be allowed to belong – even those who have been dismissed

When grave injustices are in the picture, the effects may be massive. A well-known company was getting nowhere with a subsidiary company. It turned out that Jewish owners had been forced to sell this company during the Third Reich at a ridiculously low price. (see Chapter 3.4). Seen systemically, it is no wonder that success was impossible until the founder and owner had been recognised and honoured.

There are also cases in which someone can no longer belong to the system and must be excluded, for example, because of some serious crime. When someone, such as an attorney, attempts to slander the head of the company to remove him or her from power, there are not only legal repercussions, but also systemic consequences for that person.

Those who come first have priority over those who come later

In the course of reorganisation, a new production manager takes over production. He pinpoints errors and potential cost-cutting moves, and begins cleaning out. The new head calls the work areas a disgrace, and the engineers and master workers who are responsible for it are "asleep on the job". The message is that they have almost run the company into the ground, but now the new boss is going to make a clean sweep of things. A number of sensible measures are introduced, but they don't seem to have lasting effects. The other employees are not won over. The more he encourages and spurs them on, the more lethargic and apathetic they become. What has happened?

The new boss has to lead from the last place.

The new production manager, despite good intentions, has made a serious error through his systemic ignorance. As a newcomer, he is in *last* place in the order of the system, but is acting as though he were in *first* place. The whole social system reacts violently to such presumption. On the other hand, this person is the new boss and truly wants to achieve something for the company with his competence and efforts. This requires learning to lead from the last place in the order. This is possible if he keeps in mind that many of the people in this company were producing and selling these products while he was still a schoolboy. With such a change of perspective, the newcomer's attitude changes and with it comes a change of expression and tone of voice. The performance of the others is honoured, even

27

though it may have been carried out with out-dated structures and technology. Now, in bringing in new innovative concepts, the new manager looks differently at the team leaders and master workers, asking about their experience and work habits, and requesting their opinions and ideas before making decisions. Leading from the last place wins the trust and support of his employees and allows him to fully assume a position of leadership.

Priority goes to those with more at stake in the whole

Even in teams, everyone is not equal.

Team efforts and a level hierarchy are very *"in"*. New approaches for greater effectiveness are sensible and useful, but they also harbour certain dangers. You may know of start-up teams who, in their euphoric enthusiasm confuse equal value in membership in the group with complete equality of rights. As lovely as it is to have the feeling of "we", the baby is often thrown out with the bath water in the team's attempt to level hierarchical structures. Systemic principles, such as priority for competence and responsibility, are carelessly tossed overboard. In this atmosphere, pseudo-egalitarian ideologies thrive: *"We all work together with equal rights. We are all equally important. Everyone is included in discussion and decision making."* In extreme cases, the suggestions of temp workers or interns are given equal weight to those of experienced persons in positions of responsibility.

The boss has to be the boss and lead responsibly.

In meetings of such a team, even when everyone is self-congratulatory and nodding smugly at their advanced attitudes, you can feel a certain sense of unease. Here, for those who truly carry the responsibility, there are no more "rights", only obligations. Systemically, in interpersonal systems, those who have more at stake in the whole carry more weight. This person's statements are more important. How do you get out of such a trap? One simple question brings clarity to the situation: *"Who feels responsible for the entire team and acts accordingly?"* Those who act in the interests of the whole and stand by it can develop a structure of leadership amongst themselves. The rest are team members.

Said another way – the boss has to be the boss and has to be allowed to be that. If someone rejects the role by delegating not only tasks, but also executive decision-making, he or she has already lost the position. Employees will not take such a leader seriously. On the other hand, if a team member does not acknowledge the boss as boss because he or she feels they are more competent, this person is out of kilter in the system and has to be called on it. This person, too, would benefit from acknowledging the reality of the situation, and perhaps saying to the boss, *"You are the boss here. Even though I don't always agree with you, I still recognise that."*

Competence has priority

Competence in the right place is acknowledged.

Do you know people who are competent and talented, but get little recognition for their work? This dilemma may have systemic roots. In the example we cited of "those who come first have priority", the new production manager was caught in this trap. The older workers did not respect the newcomer's competence. Only when it became clear that the rights of the long-time employees had been ignored and he had changed his attitude and approach did he begin to be accepted by the others. This example shows how various dimensions of priority exist simultaneously in a work system and are mutually dependent upon one another.

The principle of acknowledgement is critical for harmony within the system, and runs as leitmotif through all the systemic principles. When the ones who come later acknowledge those who came before, then they, in turn, willingly recognise the competence of a newcomer. One who brings a high degree of competence into the work system also has priority.

Special expertise and performance count here, just as do visible results or exceptional professional experience. Recognition and acknowledgement are basic principles of systemic balance and also a way to achieve that balance.

The Invisible Lines of Power

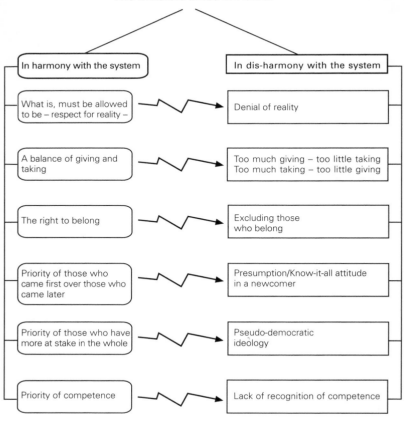

In harmony with the system	In dis-harmony with the system
What is, must be allowed to be – respect for reality –	Denial of reality
A balance of giving and taking	Too much giving – too little taking Too much taking – too little giving
The right to belong	Excluding those who belong
Priority of those who came first over those who came later	Presumption/Know-it-all attitude in a newcomer
Priority of those who have more at stake in the whole	Pseudo-democratic ideology
Priority of competence	Lack of recognition of competence

2. Systemic Constellations – Revealing Invisible Dynamics

2.1 THE DEVELOPMENT OF THIS METHOD

Developmental processes take time.

This is, perhaps, not the first time you have heard the term "systemic thinking". It is a concept that is currently in fashion, particularly in organisational development, but which has received little recognition in the business world. Why is that? Developmental processes take time – a commodity that many executives don't have, or don't take. Someone in a tight spot, who has to take immediate action, understandably has little patience. In such a situation, managers often turn to one of the "quick fix" solutions on the consulting market, which satisfy the need for action but often do not solve the problem. Pragmatism and speed will not determine the success of the measures. If you become impatient with the slow growth of a seedling, you can of course tug on it to hurry it along. The result however is that the plant is then smaller and it takes it even longer to grow.

Similar approaches are still the trend in the business world, despite a swing towards systemic thinking. Often however, the emphasis seems to be less on "systemic" and more on "thinking", but new thinking alone does not change much in practice.

Our complex business structures today are changing continuously at a whirlwind pace, and clarity cannot be simply thought into existence. New solutions require not only a change in thinking, but also concrete insights into the mechanisms at work in the system and appropriate action. This is precisely where the method of systemic constellations proves useful.

Systemic constellations are not limited to thinking; they initiate movement, and at a speed that can easily keep pace with the information technologies of "generation-@". They bring together contrasts that previously appeared incompatible. They are solution *and* pro-

31

cess orientated; they are fast *and* comprehensive; they are precise *and* symbolic. Because they demand and support precise thinking, differentiation of feelings, and consistent, appropriate action, the solutions that emerge are not rapid-fire shots in the dark, but trigger mechanisms that initiate long-term, desirable development.

How has this method evolved? As with many management approaches and models, the roots of this method lie in modern psychology and its application to human problems today. In a brief look at these origins, we would like to point out some of the correlations.

Historical development of systemic constellations

The sixties and seventies of the previous century were rich in change. They gave us the landing on the moon, the legendary ,60s generation, the Beatles and flower power. But there were also breakthroughs in our understanding of human beings and the world. To understand how fundamentally business thinking has altered, we have to look back to these psychological roots.

In psychology and social science, researchers turned away from purely quantitative, analytical dissection and suddenly saw the world through new eyes. The *whole* came into view and radically changed perspectives. New connections, reciprocal effects and bonds between people and their environment became evident. Researchers looked up from their microscopes and blinked in amazement at this new whole, which seemed to be more than the sum of its parts. It is true that ancient cultures had come to the same conclusions thousands of years ago; but now and again, we humans seem to forget what we know. Therefore, it is not wrong to say that the systemic viewpoint began in the last half of the twentieth century. In various scientific disciplines, it then developed rapidly. The sociologist Niklas Luhmann became especially well known for his theory of systems.

Origins in family therapy

The psychological researchers Gregory Bateson, Paul Watzlawick, Ronald Laing and their colleagues pressed for a more complete view of the human mind and soul. This inspired therapists such as I. Boszormenyi-Nagy, H. Stierlin and others to broaden their psychological view from the individual to include the most immediate relationship system, the family. In the field of family therapy, various schools quickly sprang up, as so often happens with new developments. Within a short time we had the Milan School, the Heidelberg School and many different approaches in America. Despite their arguments, the family therapists agreed on the following:

- The problems of the individual have to be seen in correlation with effects of the family system.
- Any behaviour, no matter how crazy it may seem, makes sense in the context of the system.
- The therapist looks towards solutions, not problems.
- Solutions are also possible in short-term therapy.

The previously psychoanalytically orientated therapy world – based on a long-term individual search for causes – was turned completely upside-down by these revolutionary new concepts.

In order to gain a better overview of the family system, family therapists began to look for ways to depict systems. At first they used graphics and figures to make the relationships between the members of the system more visible. The next step was naturally to allow the figures to speak. To get a clear picture, family members were asked to stand in relationship to one another and express themselves. When it became clear that this was too difficult, representatives were used instead. There were many experiments using various approaches. The American therapist Virginia Satir came out with her so-called "sculptures", in which she set role players in poses like living statues and let them pantomime relationships and feelings. That turned out to be rather dramatic but made it difficult to see what was essential.

Constellations reduce to the essence.
In systemic constellations of families and organisations we hold everything to a minimum.

The person who is seeking a solution or clarification of goals chooses neutral representatives for parts of an organisation or for family members. These representatives are placed in a spatial relationship to one another that reflects the person's inner sense of how things are. The reality of the interactive system is depicted symbolically, not photographically.

A constellation image is comparable to a work of art, which can present very complex contents using simple materials. We owe a lot to the pioneer work of Bert Hellinger for this non-spectacular, yet amazingly effective approach.

At this point you may be asking yourself how a method of family therapy fits in with business and your business-related questions. Businesses are not after all families, even when we are talking about a traditional small family business. Of course there are substantial differences between families and businesses, but also a number of commonalities that make it possible to adapt the systemic constellation method for use in business and organisations.

The major difference is the fact that people in your company can be fired, whereas family members cannot. Families are groups determined by fate; companies are task-orientated systems. Nonetheless businesses, like families, are human systems and therefore function according to the systemic laws and principles described in the first chapter. Working with business issues does not compare with family entanglements in terms of emotional intensity, but the procedures for the constellations are much the same.

Constellations show the situation as it is.

In both cases, a constellation is a way to quickly get an overview of the current situation as it is. In a constellation of a company, a person acting as representative for production, sales, management or a subsidiary company will be able to feel immediately whether the positioning of everyone is right in the context of the whole picture, or where changes are needed to improve the functioning of the whole. Existing situations that are difficult will be experienced as tense – good resolutions will produce a relaxation of that tension. Anyone can enter into this experience in the role of representative, and it is surprisingly easy for most people. It is as simple as seeing and hearing, and is not dependent upon any particular training or qualifications. In this chapter in part 2.3 you will find a more complete explanation of this phenomenon.

2.2 Two paths to the same goal: Solutions

Focus on solutions

It is clearly an advantage to have access to an overview of a current situation within an hour. Nothing else can beat that for speed; what traditional method of business analysis could do this well? However that is not all. The real purpose for doing a constellation is to find solutions, not just analysis and research. Systemic consultants do not ask *"Why did the company managers react so slowly to changes in the market?"* Or, *"Why are the development and sales departments so poorly coordinated?"* The systemic questions are more likely to be: *"How can we get on top of the current crisis and move into a strategic market position?"* Or, *"How can we organise ourselves in a way that will help us react more quickly to changes?"*

Constellations are geared towards practical application.
The difference in the way the questions are formulated makes it clear that the interest here is not in assigning blame for the problems, which is often what happens with a "why?" question. The "how?" questions are more helpful. *"How can we do this better?"*

What you need is the right solution, the optimal line-up formation for your team! It is not unlike football; even the best players cannot win if problems in the team system counteract their efforts.

Suddenly passes that have been practiced to perfection cannot be completed and the strikers are unable to move forward into the lucrative goal area. They are trapped back in their own half, trying to help the defence fight off the opponents' gains. How does a football coach find the optimal line-up? Whether a top coach operates in secretive silence, or lets loose in verbal fireworks is a question of his sales presentation. The magical formula in the background is always the same, *look towards solutions.* The orientation is not towards the problem but towards the goals, the solution.

The questions at the beginning of a systemic constellation are therefore, *"What would you like to achieve?"* and, *"How will you be able to tell if the situation has improved?"* With this concrete, practical orientation, the final image at the end of a systemic constellation can turn the stress of a problem situation into energy for action.

Do we invent reality?
In systemic work, two different approaches have developed, both with an orientation towards solutions. The first operates under the name of *"constructivism"*, the other is known as *"phenomenology"*. Constructivists are of the opinion that reality is, so to speak, invented and constructed by individuals. Phenomenologists do not contradict this position, but expand the notion of reality to include a larger whole, which we do not create but rather discover. Therefore they

look at a system without preconceptions and with no intent to change it, but simply as an unknown phenomenon.

The phenomenologists maintain that before we can opt for solutions we have to be cognisant of reality and acknowledge it as it is. System dynamics are similar to the physical laws of nature, which are known for resisting our efforts to change them. The goal is to find solutions that are in harmony with the fundamental principles in the whole system. Succinctly stated, phenomenologists look at the central issue of "what is"; constructivists look at the imagined concept of "what could be".

The constructivist viewpoint

When a business is doing poorly, the constructivist view is that this is a result of certain thoughts, worries for example, that those in the company share with one another, thereby strengthening the negative images over time until finally an external result appears (for example a drop in productivity). Naturally this serves as evidence to justify the worries. The constructivist solution would be for the people in the company to choose a better, more successful reality and achieve it in the same way. In the constructivist view, all the resources for the solution are already available within the system; they have just been forgotten in some unused area and can be activated with the help of a systemic advisor. This person's task is to stimulate and support the collective creation of a new common reality.

The phenomenological viewpoint

Their colleagues who are working phenomenologically will first look for places where the systemic principles are being violated and will bring these into order.

Denying reality weakens. Acknowledging reality strengthens.

Therefore phenomenologists encourage those involved to first acknowledge reality. From this viewpoint, a conflict between two departments cannot be solved by the department heads getting together to work out cooperative strategies for working together. No, first it has to be made clear where the conflict is. Descriptions by the individuals involved may cover up the actual issue rather than clarifying it. This is one reason for doing constellations with neutral representatives instead of with those who are actually involved.

A conflict between sales and production

Assume the problem is something similar to the conflict between the sales manager and the production manager. The latter feels passed over by the salesperson in the critical planning stages; the head of sales feels unappreciated for his or her efforts on behalf of the whole company. In a constellation of the situation, the coach suggests short dialogues that will acknowledge reality.

Sales to Production: You are the head of production here and you're responsible for the whole production line. Without your efforts, we wouldn't be able to sell anything!
Production to Sales: Our jobs depend on your success as head of sales. I recognise that!

When those involved acknowledge the position and responsibility of each other, they can work out the details of their future work together.

What is right, constructivism or phenomenology? *Both* are right. With a new construct, the constructivist approach shows a path to the implementation of solutions. The phenomenological contribution of the basic principles of the system complements the other method by pointing out the realistic limits of the applicability of solutions. Briefly summarised: Solutions are possible and new goals reachable, but not without certain limits – they can only work if they are in harmony with the principles of systems.

2.3 How does a systemic constellation function?

Let us turn to the practice. How does this method function? What actually happens in a constellation?

A clear issue is a basic requirement.

First of all, in order to use this method there must be a clearly defined issue. At the least, you have to notice where the shoe is rubbing and be clear about the fact that you would like to change this situation so that your feet no longer hurt. Or, perhaps you have no real problem but there is a goal you would like to reach and you want to find out what will be needed to do this. You can get clearer about the factors in a difficult decision by using a special constellation form.

A systemic coach will help you to find a precise formulation of your issue, because this method will not function if the issue is not clear. If there is not a clear issue, the energy and the orientation (solution, goals) are missing. That would be something like getting into a taxi and saying, *"Let's go."* The taxi driver would ask where you wanted to go and you would answer, *"It doesn't matter. I'm needed everywhere."*

A qualified coach

The next thing you need is a "cab driver" who knows the territory, that is, a constellation leader who is competent to do the job. This is particularly important because a constellation looks very simple from the outside and seems as if it could be technically very easily replicated. It is however an extremely complex task in which there are different levels of awareness that must all be attended to simultaneously. This demands a solid basis of training and experience. In section 2.5, we will present what we feel is essential to assure competence in a coach or trainer in systemic constellation work.

It is easiest with neutral representatives.

The third thing needed is a group of representatives for the people, goals, issues or functions involved in your issue. It is easiest to do a constellation using representatives who have no connection to the issue, and no knowledge of the internal workings of your company system. These could be participants in an open seminar. If that is not available, it may be possible to use people from the organisation, but each taking a role of someone or something else, not his or her own position. As a double check against false information, for example, personal considerations or animosity, you can ask various individuals to stand in one role, one after the other. If there are neither external nor internal representatives available, or if the nature of the issue demands that it be handled with secrecy, a constellation can be done in an individual session with your coach using figures, cards or floor markers to designate the positions.

Only the facts

If you are working with representatives, it is important that they receive only the information that is absolutely necessary and nothing else. This means the external facts:

- What person/position am I representing?
- Who are the other people/positions in the constellation?

In addition, the coach needs the following basic information:

- What does this company do, exactly? (What does it develop, produce, or sell?)
- What is the hierarchy in the organisation? (If necessary, this information can be outlined in an organisational chart for clarification.)
- What critical developments have occurred (founding, takeovers, mergers, reorganising measures, restructuring, downsizing, booms, product changes)?

While gathering this information, the coach has to be alert to any interpretations or value judgments about people or events to prevent the representatives from being influenced in any particular direction.

Assuming you have representatives on hand, the first step is for the constellation leader to decide with you, which people or parts of the system (subsidiaries, branches, departments, customers, market, and so on) are essential to begin with. You will then be asked to choose a representative from those present to represent each: for example, a representative for the boss, one for the customers, someone for the sales team and a representative for you, yourself. It is not necessary to give much thought to which person would be the best for which role. You do not need to look for a person with executive qualities to represent the boss. One person is as good as any other in reporting sensations in the role. If possible, choose women for female roles and men for male positions. Your coach will then ask you to proceed without speaking, in a collected manner, and take each representative lightly by the shoulders and position them somewhere in the space available. The representatives should stand in a relationship to one another that corresponds to your inner image of the situation.

In the placement of representatives in a constellation, you are creating a symbolic, three-dimensional picture that reflects your own inner image of the relationship structures.

A "collected" state is important in setting up a constellation.

It is basically easy to do, but requires a bit of preparation beforehand if you have never done this before. What does it mean to do something in a "collected" manner and what is an "inner image"? Being collected means having all five senses at your disposal. Your awareness is tuned to all the sensory input available at any given moment. You notice how you are standing and how you are breathing; at the same time you hear noises in your surroundings and see the people in the room and the room itself. At the beginning of a constellation group we practice this kind of attentive awareness. In a collected state it is easier to follow your inner image and feelings and to place the representatives intuitively, without thinking too rationally about it.

EQ leads to the goal.

A constellation is not a *chess match*, in which you proceed in a logical and considered manner, but it is also not *mind-mapping* all your creative ideas. You call up your *emotional intelligence*, which allows you to trust and follow your awareness of the moment. Emotional intelligence, your "EQ", is a resource from the right half of the brain that is attracting increasing interest in the field of business. Thanks to this potential you can be totally aware. This facility allows you to reach your goals, not through careful analytic planning and logical steps, but in one leap to the desired finish line. As you follow your intuitive insights, an image, a completed gestalt, opens up and lights up the unknown dark areas.

Right brain intelligence

Many great discoveries, from the light bulb to the theory of relativity, have occurred to inventors in this way, but intuitive intelligence is not limited to geniuses. We all have a right brain and can tap our creative potential using the simple instrument of systemic constellations to resolve complex problems. One advantage is that we circumvent language.

Using words, we can describe a situation only sequentially, in dissected fragments. An image however encompasses the whole. Using other methods you would have to ask many questions, analyse, check things out and ask more questions in order to even come close to the information offered by a single constellation image.

40

If you are feeling sceptical, remain so! The basis of the word "sceptic" contains the idea of looking carefully at something with thoughtful consideration. What is called for here is a non-biased consideration of actual sensory awareness, not a belief system – in other words, scepticism.

You observe yourself in your work system.

When the representatives have been positioned with care, the coach will ask you to remove yourself to a seat outside the constellation where you can follow the proceedings as an observer. Grochowiak et. al. explain the reasons for this step:

When the client has externalised an inner sense of things, he or she retreats to the role of observer and the representatives act as a mirror of the patterns of relationship, needs and emotions in the client's system.

This gives you the opportunity of observing from the outside your own role in your work system. The representatives portray the various roles without the bias of those personally involved because they have only been given the minimum of factual information necessary to take on the role.

Systemic dynamics become visible.

In the first phase the coach stays open to the impact of the first image, paying close attention to the non-verbal reactions of the representatives. The coach may ask representatives to follow through on any impulse they might feel to move in a particular direction, thereby altering the initial picture. Then the representatives are asked to report their sensations and experience of the situation. Their feedback and their positions within the designated space will reveal the dynamics of the system. The crucial information becomes clear to the observers by the direction the representatives are facing, their distance from one another, and their positions, individually and in relation to others. For example the representative for the new managing director might be looking at the employees with little sense of respect. They in turn are ignoring the new boss, their loyalties still with the old boss who was let go in the merger. In the grip of these dynamics, both have lost sight of the customers whose representative is standing there confused and annoyed.

According to G. Weber, one of the values of the constellation method is that it raises our awareness of precisely such everyday dynamics.

Processes like these occur constantly in everyday life, but remain outside of our awareness and attention, or are regarded as meaningless ... In the concentrated work of a constellation, they are given a place. They appear and unfold and are given the weight and importance they have previously been denied. (G. Weber)

Before we continue with the procedures of the constellation, we will give you an example of some of the most common systemic dynamics. In Chapter 3 you will find case studies that illuminate these dynamics.

Loyalty

During a critical phase, the boss has to relinquish control to an external manager. The employees, consciously or unconsciously, remain loyal to the old boss. At whatever level of awareness, they reject the new boss and act in ways that contribute to his or her failure. A similar dynamic appears when a colleague is unfairly dismissed or squeezed out of the organisation and those who are left remain loyal to their less fortunate colleagues. On behalf of the one who has been treated unfairly, they sabotage any projects of the "guilty" party,

Taking over

Better me than you

The dynamics of someone "taking over" can best be understood in the context of the family. A child senses an emergency, for example, that the father of the family is ill. The child wants to take over the burden. At a deep level the child says, *"Better me than you. Better that I become ill. Better that I should suffer than you."*

In the magical thinking of a child, the little one believes that his or her own suffering will relieve the father's illness and suffering. This kind of thinking continues at an unconscious level into adulthood and extends into other relationships.

These dynamics are particularly important in family businesses, but can appear even when there are no family connections. The head of a company may unconsciously believe that he or she should not be successful as long as the affiliate company is operating in the red. Without any conscious awareness, this take-over pattern from childhood is carried over to a business – as if it were possible to balance someone else's misfortune with voluntary self-sacrifice.

Projection

It may happen that someone gets their boss confused with their father. Feelings that actually belong in a child-parent relationship are projected on to a work relationship. This becomes particularly problematic when the employee is or was in a position of taking something over from father in his or her own family. The pattern may be repeated in the work situation and individuals unconsciously create problems for themselves or their department as if that would relieve problems elsewhere.

Presumption

Inappropriate positions

Through some unconscious confusion, one person in the system may take over a position that is not rightfully theirs. The head of a department might repeatedly take over control in other departments, assuming a competence that is not really there. These dynamics are usually seen in people who have taken over an inappropriate role in their own family. One distortion commonly seen in families is when children become the advisors and cohorts of one parent against the other.

Representation

Unintentional failure

When a group of owners or shareholders make a large profit at the cost of others in the company, one of the "winners" may feel moved to represent those who went empty handed. This "representative" unconsciously tries to achieve balance by suffering a major loss as punishment. Occasionally such a "representative" can provoke failure in a whole branch of the company. They are representing the conscience of the system. The same dynamics show up when employees intentionally allow their boss to fail, because of unfair treatment of a co-worker, or sabotage colleagues who have harassed a member of the team. This kind of systemic "guilt" demands compensation but is not to be confused with moral guilt.

"This guilt is removed from ethical judgements and is to be understood in an economic sense. Compensation is required from the guilty party, but that person is not seen as "bad". Systemic guilt as a need for balance and

recompense allows a stabilisation of the system that would be impossible with any designation of ethical guilt. The economic sense of guilt is closer to the idea of debt than it is to evil ..." (Sparrer / Varga von Kibèd)

Physical sensations as a seismograph

When the basic dynamics of the system have become clear, the coach begins to reorganise the placement of the representatives in response to their feeling of whether a position feels "better" or "worse". If there is no substantial, clear feedback, the leader continues to test out various possibilities until there is a clear positive or negative signal.

It often happens that a representative responds to a new position with astonishing relief and reports that a heavy burden has been removed, or that the person can suddenly breathe freely again, or they finally feel free to make contact with another representative. For those who are taking part in a constellation for the first time, it is often new and surprising when they discover that they can physically feel something that has nothing to do with them personally. The physical reaction of a representative acts like a seismograph for the positive or negative effects of various positions in the system.

Using this kind of feedback, constellation leaders are able to steer the system's ship, so to speak, through the fog of the problems into the port of the solutions.

We do not know why the awareness of neutral individuals should be able to channel such precise information, but it has been confirmed thousands of times by countless representatives – sceptics as well as supporters of the method.

For a closer look at the beginnings of a scientific discussion of this phenomenon, we refer you to the work of the English biologist Rupert Sheldrake.

Acknowledging what is

Sometimes a resolution demands that a representative in a difficult position acknowledge and utter aloud certain realities of the system: *"You were in this company long before me." "You belong here." "I recognise your competence."* The coach formulates such resolving or relieving statements based on his or her awareness of the system. The representatives check out whether the statements feel ,right' before they accept the formulation. That is easy to do, even for beginners, because they can feel immediately whether a statement has a relieving effect in their role or not.

Finding a better order using feedback and repositioning

Gradually, using the verbal and non-verbal feedback of the representatives, the coach will discover the optimal positioning of the system, one that brings it into "order". You know that the correct order of the system has been achieved when everyone involved is standing in an appropriate place and experiences it as "right". There is often a hierarchical organisation from right to left in a constellation. The more important and influential a person or position is in the system, the further to the right that person stands in the constellation. The founder and the chief executive of a company would stand furthest to the right. To the left, the system is arranged either according to hierarchy (importance for the survival of the system) or according to seniority (time of belonging to the system). It does not matter whether this is in the form of a half-circle, a row or some other arrangement.

The configuration of resolution is checked carefully.

The leader of the constellation continually checks the individual steps by asking the client for more information. The feedback from the client about his or her experience in the company is often remarkably close to the statements of the representatives. When the final image of resolution has been reached, it is clear to everyone involved. They immediately feel the effects of this constellation as a relief, a support, or as a feeling of readiness for something new. The last step is for you the client to step into the constellation in place of your representative so that you can personally experience the configuration of the solution, check it against your sense of the issue, and take in the image to hold and take away with you.

Only as much as is necessary

So that a solution can be found with the most effective use of time and energy, we do not usually set up a constellation of a complete system. We look at only those pieces that are necessary at the moment for a solution and then add additional factors if and when they are needed.

Thanks to the creative spirit of Insa Sparrer and Matthias Varga von Kibèd, we have many different forms of constellation at our disposal for use in groups of representatives or on a one-to-one basis. From their book on the basic forms of constellations of systemic structures, we have also taken a summary of some of the steps of a constellation.

Summary of steps in a systemic constellation

- *A clearly defined issue from the client. What, precisely, do I want to achieve?*
- *Choice of the level of the system to be addressed (company, department, team), and choice of the constellation approach (goal constellation, problem constellation, company culture constellation or other).*
- *Choice of representatives for persons, themes or functions.*
- *A collected and considered placement of the representatives.*
- *Review and check of the configuration by the client.*
- *Intervention based on non-verbal feedback of the representatives, possibly an alteration in the constellation based on representatives' impulses for movement.*
- *Feedback from representatives about their awareness and experience.*
- *Crosscheck of this feedback with the client.*
- *Re-positioning in the constellation by coach.*
- *Feedback from representatives (better or worse).*
- *Additional changes in positioning or process work (dialogues, resolving statements) until a constellation or image of resolution has been reached.*
- *Client's experience of the configuration of resolution (replaces own representative).*
- *Checking the image of resolution against the initial issue. Corrections where needed.*
- *Anchoring the image of resolution as a starting point for the resolving process in actual life.*
- *Releasing representatives from their roles. Additional feedback.*
- *Follow-up discussion.*

2.4 WHEN IS A SYSTEMIC CONSTELLATION USEFUL?

You may be wondering at this point whether this method is appropriate for your business situation or for you and your issue personally. For which concrete questions can a constellation be used with good results? A practical example:

Things are not going well in the company. Customers are leaving, business is dropping off and the mood is down. What is wrong?

All the usual analyses have been done with no real progress. Anxiety begins to creep through the system and leads to tension and tighter controls. Drastic financial reorganisation is considered to cut costs and concentrate on core skills by out-sourcing. Such concepts rarely take into consideration how the system, the organism of the company, will react to these measures. In positive cases, the workers and management stand behind the measures and support the strategy for handling the crisis; the storm sails are hoisted and the company ship sails through the waves like the Flying Dutchman, clearing the rocks.

What are the chances for financial reorganisation?

Why does the company sometimes react to an effort at financial reorganisation like an immune system reacting to an infection? The reasons for such a reaction are seldom to be found at the economic, business level. More often, systemic orders have been disrupted. The company heads have changed direction without consulting the compass. They would have had to first ask, *"What is our employees' orientation? What is their attitude towards the company? In what situations have we previously got their support and involvement? What values have contributed to success in the past? What do they need in order to understand and support our measures?"*

In this case systemic constellations can help to clarify which measures are in keeping with the company system and which are not. They also give indications about the positioning of company employees, acceptance on the part of the customers and potential dangers in the market. In this way you can avoid costly mistakes and mobilise resources. As G. Weber points out, constellations provide a risk-free trial run and are well suited for trying out one possible solution after another.

In the following checklist we have summarised additional examples of possible applications, using brief questions. For the purpose of a constellation, the issues would have to be more precisely defined in terms of a solution orientation.

Checklist for possible applications
Gathering information about important personnel and economic decisions
  – Is applicant A or B better suited to us?
  – How can a team structure function in our organisation? How does it have to be set up so that projects run smoothly?

- Is a cooperative effort possible with company XY?
- Can we rely on our foreign affiliate if we alter products?
- Are the areas of competence and responsibility in the company clearly defined?
- Have we got the right number of people working in department Y?

Recognising the dynamics of an organisation (coalitions, competition, etc.)
- What is going wrong between delivery and purchasing?
- Why does development have such a poor image in the company?
- Why is the position of sales manager such a hot seat?
- What is blocking the flow of information in the company?
- Why do people keep quitting in department B?
- Why is everybody complaining about quality control?

Checking out and optimising the leadership functions in the company
- What is the position of the new managing director in the system?
- How can cooperation between branch managers be improved?
- How can we integrate up-and-coming leaders in a good way?
- What would bring clarity to our leadership structure?
- What effect do the interests of the shareholders have on our company culture?

Recognising which resources are needed and where
- What is preventing us from being successful in market segment Z?
- How can we strengthen our core capabilities?
- How can we improve our internal procedures between A and B?
- What is behind the sluggish sales of product X?
- What would improve contact with our customers?
- How can we get our goals back in sight?

Developing a company culture
- What role do values, visions and goals actually play in our company?
- How do the employees view management concepts?

- Who formally runs the business? Who runs it informally?
- What would it take to weld our team together?
- What is the basis of the conflict between new employees and old-timers?
- What is the status of trust and loyalty in the company?
- How attractive is this company for new employees?

Finding the right place as an outside consultant
- What is my place as a consultant in this company?
- What is blocking progress in my consulting?
- Am I allowing myself to be pulled into the company? Is my task clearly defined?
- What do I need to be accepted by my customers?
- How can I successfully expand?

Attaining personal goals
- What do I need in order to attain my career goals?
- Am I in the right place in my company?
- Should I be considering changing companies, or should I be thinking about becoming self-employed?
- What would bring my personal goals into line with my professional goals?
- How can I successfully and fairly mediate conflicts?

2.5 WHAT SKILLS ARE NEEDED TO LEAD CONSTELLATIONS?

The right attitude for exactitude

Even though titles such as "trainer" or "coach" do not exactly fit in with the method of systemic constellations, we are using these terms for constellation leaders because the work is primarily done by trainers. What skills should a trainer have? What kind of background and understanding is helpful? A constellation looks very simple. Among other things, this is what makes it so interesting. It depicts reality in a highly concentrated, symbolic form, much like a work of art that makes complex relationships clear at a single glance. An observer who relies on the left half of the brain and looks at the process purely logically and analytically sees only a positioning and repositioning, and hears only set, pat-sounding formulations. Such an observer may wonders what exactly is happening, a new role-play? A kind of company theatre, perhaps? As long as the intuitive, right-brain emotional intelligence is not allowed to function, there will be no apparent rhyme or reason. But when it is allowed in, it will be as if someone had been standing in a forest, recognising only cubic metres of lumber. Suddenly he realises that the forest is alive. He identifies a fascinating and extremely complex biological system. He might even experience something like wonder. Something similar happens with human systems. The intentions of the members, their connections and interconnections, and the subtle effects of all those are only disclosed to us when we allow it to affect us intuitively through the right brain, like a painting or a sculpture.

A constellation leader needs inner and outer experience.
What looks very simple demands, in actual practice, a multitude of training skills and experience. It is similar to some kinds of arts or sports. When you watch a master of the art, you might be tempted to think at first, *"I could do that!"* The error of your thinking becomes quickly apparent as soon as you try to do it yourself. A famous sculptor was once asked how he managed to turn a formless block of stone into such a wonderfully expressive statue. He answered, *"That's very simple. I just knock off all the stone bits that don't belong to the statue."* Absolutely simple! Although there are also tools to be mastered in systemic constellations, it is less a question of learning a craft as it is a matter of developing the skill of maintaining a particular inner attitude. An old Chinese story illustrates the difference between technical perfection and an inner stance.

The best archer in the land, unconquerable by anyone, heard of an old archery master who lived as a hermit high in the mountains. Curious to see if he could win a contest with him, the archer set out to find the hermit. The old man greeted him in a friendly manner, whereupon the younger archer demonstrated his skill straight away. He hung a target the size of a small saucer on a tree at a distance of 50 metres, put a cup brimming with water on his outstretched arm and shot off three arrows. All three arrows hit the target and not a drop of water was spilled. The old man smiled. "You shoot well. You have a steady hand. But, can you count on it?" He led his visitor to a cliff towering precipitously hundreds of metres above a chasm. He stood on the outermost edge of the overhang with his back to the drop-off. Calm and relaxed, with only the balls of his feet on solid ground, he appeared to be hanging in thin air out over the abyss. "Come here!" he challenged his would-be opponent. "Take your bow, stand here next to me and perform your trick again." The young archer cowered on the ground in front of him as if paralysed. He trembled and sweated with fear and realised that his technical skill did not ensure a steady hand.

> *Technical skill alone is not enough.*

If technical skill is not enough, then what is?

Although not to such extremes, a constellation leader, like the old Chinese man, needs an inner calm, a sense of being collected and a steady hand. The critical system dynamics operate unseen and become visible only when one is able to put aside all intention and allow the effects of the constellation to penetrate.

As Hellinger explained, when we say the leader is to put aside all intentions, it does not mean an attitude of "it's all the same to me". It means that whatever a constellation reveals is equally valid.

"This way of knowing demands an emptiness in regard to previous expectations as well as in terms of inner movements ... Your attention is both focused and unfocused, collected." (Hellinger)

In practice, this stance of impartiality is important for a constellation leader in order to keep from siding with one party or another. In our experience, it is easy for misinterpretations to occur if a trainer or coach has not worked through his or her own personal and family systems. Therefore we consider it absolutely obligatory for constellation leaders who work with businesses and organisations to also have prepared themselves through personal work and experience with family constellations. The latter is particularly important because certain topics in business overlap with family dynamics. For example, if a company director repeatedly overlooks dangerous risks, it is often helpful to check out whether there are parallels in his or her family (naturally only with the consent of the person involved and in an appropriate setting). If someone becomes aware of such problematic dynamics in their own family, they will be able to act more cautiously in business situations in the future. Just as important as the trainer's skill and experience is the "chemistry" between the trainer and the participants. This has to feel right if their cooperative efforts are to succeed.

3. Systemic Constellations in Practice – Case Examples

In this chapter we invite you to participate vicariously in organisation constellations through examples taken from case studies.

After each constellation you will be given information about the system dynamics at work in this case, what violations of basic systemic principles allowed the problem to arise and to escalate, and how the image of resolution can be applied in practice.

For better understanding we have described the steps in the first example in detail. In the subsequent cases we have presented the steps more briefly.

In order for you to get a complete picture, we have included a detailed account of background information in each case example. In actual practice it is not necessary to have this much background information before working with a systemic constellation; you need only the bare facts in order to find a systemic solution to a complex problem. In fact, representatives find it easier to get a good feeling for a role when they do not know the details of the situation. The privacy of the client is also protected. The case studies have come from our seminars and consulting projects. For the protection of our clients we have altered the identifying details, so that any resemblance to actual persons or companies is purely coincidental.

3.1 "WE ARE LOSING OUR BEST PEOPLE!" DIRECTOR OF A MEDIUM-SIZED COMPANY FIGHTS HIGH EMPLOYEE TURNOVER AND INTERNAL RESISTANCE

Background information

This family business, with about 3,000 employees, looks back on a turbulent history. The company was originally founded by the boss's father. The boss himself has been a model and orientation point for all the employees. The products manufactured by this company so strongly carried the stamp of his personality that one could say that he embodied the essence of the company. It is no wonder then that the employees identified strongly with their boss. They had been through the good years and the bad years together. In the eighties there were times when an export boom gave the company an unprecedented boost. During that period, the number of employees in development and production almost doubled. The boss and his managerial team showed their appreciation by awarding their employees top salaries and premiums.

Crisis in the company ...

As the dollar exchange dropped, the export boom came to an abrupt halt, and hard times set in. The management team continued production, keeping on all employees as long as it was at all possible. Soon it reached the point where expenses forced the management to let many employees go; even the board of directors was not immune to consequences. The old boss stepped down and turned the chair over to an external manager, a man who had been sought out because of his reputation for successful financial reorganisation.

... leads to downsizing.

The new man began to restructure the company from the ground up. With a name change, the founder's name slipped into the background. Many in management were replaced with new people chosen by the new director, and he proceeded down through the levels of the company in the same way. In the course of the downsizing, entire levels of the previous hierarchy were eliminated, increased productivity was demanded, premiums were dropped and recognition for achievement was no longer forthcoming. What had been exceptional efforts of the employees on behalf of their company were now taken for granted.

Shocked by the massive impact their company had sustained and fearing for their jobs, everyone continued working as before, but grimly. They still felt supported by a sense of solidarity that had been forged in the time of crisis, so they initially accepted the hard conditions without a murmur.

As a result, the efforts of the new management were initially rewarded by success. Costs were drastically reduced, production time shortened, warehouse stock reduced to a minimum and considerable savings made on materials. In short, it did not take long before the company, with its reduced staff, was functioning profitably again.

However, the first flush of success soon faded as new problems began to arise. The previously enthusiastic customers began to lose interest in the company's products and analyses traced this back to the less expensive, but poorer quality materials. When improvements in the quality of materials brought no real change, management went into a skid. In the meantime they had begun numerous new projects and, for one line of products, they had already completed the development phase and built two new factories.

High employee turnover

Although market research prognoses were pessimisstic, the new boss continued along the same course. The crisis spread. In the key departments of development and production there was an extremely high turnover of qualified engineers. To fill the gaps, management lured new applicants with high salaries, which meant that newcomers were earning considerably more than their more experienced colleagues. Even more workers handed in their notice and left, and older workers retreated into an inner, if not actual, termination.

Systemically orientated intervention

The turnover in personnel was very distressing to Mr P, the head of development. *"We're losing our best people and they're the ones we desperately need."* His area of responsibility in software engineering was particularly hard hit by the wave of changes, so he was the one to seize the initiative and consulted with us about ways of putting a stop to this high staff turnover.

Mr P agreed to our suggestion of a constellation of the organisation as a first step towards getting a complete picture of the current situation and looking for possible solutions. We invited him to participate in an open seminar for systemic organisation constellations that would have the advantage of doing the constellation with neutral representatives.

The next step: The constellation

With the help of the coach, Mr P formulated his issue for the constellation: *"My goal is to get a grip on the high personnel turnover and to make our product attractive to our customers again."*

He then chose a representative from the group of participants for each of the following people or positions.

Person/Position	Represented in the Constellation by
Mr P, himself	A representative, referred to as "Mr P"
The new boss	A representative
The employees	One representative for all the employees
The customers	One representative for all the customers
The products	One representative for all the products

When he had chosen all the representatives and "collected" himself, he placed the representatives in their positions and returned to his chair to observe the proceedings.

To place the representatives in a "collected" way means:

The person setting up the constellation (the client) guides the representatives, one after another, to a place that fits the client's inner image in terms of the relationships between them and the distance they stand from one another. This is done without speaking; the representatives simply allow themselves to be guided to their position.

At this point the coach and representatives take over.

In this example, we would like to show you every important step of a constellation: the first configuration, which shows the situation as it stands, the ensuing images which reflect the work in process, and the image of resolution.

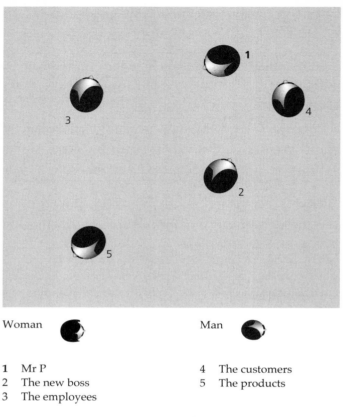

Woman   Man

1   **Mr P**   4   The customers
2   The new boss   5   The products
3   The employees

Fig. 1: The situation as it is

This is the way the representatives were placed in the working space.

- *The customers* (Position 4): The representative of the customers is turned away, looking at a point outside the constellation.
- *The employees* (Position 3): The representative of the employees is to the side, on a line with Mr P, looking the same direction as the customers.
- *The new boss* (Position 2): The representative of the new boss is
  positioned centrally, looking at the customers.
- *Mr P* (Position 1): His representative is standing between the
  new boss and the spot the customers and the employees are
  focused on. He is facing the employees.

– *The products* (Position 5): The representative of the products is standing off to the side with his back turned to the rest.

We allow this image work on us for a bit and give the representatives some time to feel their way into their roles.

Anyone can take on a representative role without any special preparation or skills. However as with many things in life, "practice makes perfect". That means that each time someone takes on a representative role it becomes easier to get into the role of a stranger. It is frequently possible to actually see the role being "taken in" as the posture and expressions of the representative change; sometimes there are visible signs of an urge to move in some way.

We gather first impressions from the representatives by asking them, *"How is this for you here in this position? What and who are you aware of? Do you feel any urge to move?"* The answers help to make the dynamics of the current situation visible.

We begin with the representative for Mr P.

Mr P

Coach: How are you feeling here?
Mr P: I don't feel well! I'm very tense. The only thing that interests me is the employees and I'm looking at them. It disturbs me that everyone is looking in a different direction.

The employees

Coach: How is the representative of the employees doing?
Employees: I'm looking off into the distance. I am hardly aware of anything else. I feel some connection to him (points to the representative for Mr P). Over in the direction of the new boss it's rather cool. I feel a very definite urge to move in the direction I'm looking in.

The new boss

Coach: What do you notice?
New boss: Like Mr P, I also feel disturbed that everyone is looking in a different direction.
Coach: Are you looking at anyone?
New boss: Yes, I keep feeling drawn to look over at the customers. They are important to me. I can't say any more than that at the moment.

The customers

Coach: How is the representative of the customers feeling?
Customers: I'm looking off into the distance. I feel drawn to something out there. (He indicates the same direction the employees are looking.) Nothing else interests me at the moment.

The products

Coach: How is the representative of the products doing?
Products: I feel completely pushed aside over here. I don't know what's going on behind my back. It makes me furious! After all, this company is nothing without me! I would be happy to move even further out.
Coach: Follow your impulse and move.
(The representative of the products moves further away from the others. He nods. "That's better.")

At this point we ask for a reaction from Mr P, who has observed the process from outside the constellation.

Coach: What do you have to say to that? Does this have any meaning for you – what has been said and what you have seen?
Mr P: Yes. This looks very familiar to me. Just like my representative, I could feel the tension from the employees. It's a frightening picture, that no one is aware of anyone else. I've never felt that to such a degree in the company. What does it mean that the two representatives, the customers and the employees, are looking off into the distance? That's very strange!
Coach: That will be our next step, to find out what the customers and the employees are looking at. I have a hunch and we're going to check it out.

What the employees and customers are looking at

We ask Mr P to choose an additional representative from the group of participants. To begin with, we refer to this representative merely as *"what the customers and employees are looking at"*. Mr P positions the new representative at the place where the representatives of the customers and employees have been looking. This creates the first process picture.

The work in process – interim pictures

What follows is a series of pictures, the steps leading to the image of resolution. We have chosen this format in order to quickly present the essence of the process and dialogue, which in practice can take up to an hour to complete.

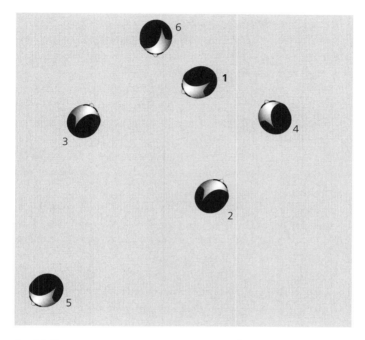

1	Mr P	4	The customers
2	The new boss	5	The products
3	The employees	6	The old boss

Fig. 2: In process

Facing one another, the employees, the customers and the new representative (*what the customers and employees are looking at* – position 6) now begin to smile at each other. In answer to the coach's question about what has changed, they reply, "It's good to see him, whoever he is."

At this point we check out our hypothesis.

Coach (to representative of the employees); Would you please say to this new representative, "For us you are still the heart and soul of the company."?

When asked if that felt "right" to them both, they both nod and exhale in relief. We take this as a sign that our intervention is moving in the right direction, and it is now clear that the new representative is standing for the *old boss*.

We ask the new representative to tell the employees, *"I'm sorry that I had to leave you."* The representative of the employees nods and indicates non-verbally that it is good to hear this.

"Sentences that resolve", usually suggestions from the coach, are one of the tools for systemic process work. By checking them out against feedback from the representatives, it is clear whether a particular sentence has a relieving effect or not.

The representative of the customers expresses a newly awakened interest in the old boss. *"When you're there, I start getting interested in the products again."*

The inclusion of the old boss in the constellation picture, as well as the formulation and expression of resolving sentences between the *old boss, customers* and *employees,* relieves some of the tension that was so clearly visible in the first image.

Interestingly enough, the representative of the *products* had already begun shifting his weight from side to side and when asked, says that he feels an urge to turn around and move in closer. The employees, customers and new boss also want to turn around so they can see the *products.* A new picture emerges in the process.

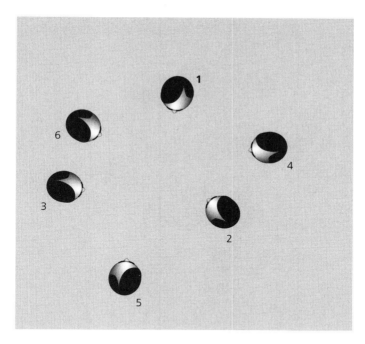

1 Mr P
2 The new boss
3 The employees
4 The customers
5 The products
6 The old boss

Fig. 3: Second picture in process

We ask the employees, customers and the new boss to turn around and we place the products so that the representative can be seen by the others. The representative of the products feels recognised and in the "right" place. The customers and employees begin to look at him with interest.

The old boss feels something is missing to his left. He says he feels "an emptiness". We choose an additional representative and provisionally put him in the constellation to the left of the old boss, as a representative for the *employees who were dismissed* during the crisis period (position 7). The configuration presents the next picture in the process.

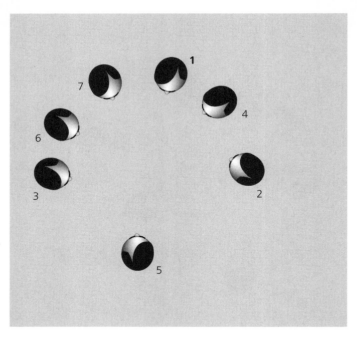

1	Mr P	5	The products
2	The new boss	6	The old boss
3	The employees	7	Dismissed employees
4	The customers		

Fig. 4: Third picture in process

This feels better to the representative of the old boss. The *dismissed employees* (position 7) look at him with sympathy. The employees and the old boss both turn towards the dismissed employees and say to them, *"You have a place here. Without your sacrifice, we wouldn't have survived."* The representative for the dismissed employees had previously reported a feeling of heaviness, but he now feels relieved.

We return to Mr P, who has been watching the changes very intensely from his outside position.

Coach: Have you got any questions or is there anything you would like to add?

Mr P: What I am seeing here gives me a lot to think about. If this is right, then some things have really gone awry with us. But could that have these sorts of effects?

Coach: It looks like what we are seeing here are the dynamics of the employee turnover and customer response to your products.

The coach turns to the representative of the *new boss* (position 2). He appears increasingly nervous. He says he would like to change his position and leave the constellation. In the context of a constellation this usually means that he wants to get out of the system, in this case the company.

The new boss

He follows his impulse, turns away and leaves the circle. Then he hesitates, turns around again and comes back.

Coach: What is happening for you? Are you being pulled away from the company?

New boss: At first, that's what I wanted to do, but then it didn't feel right. But there is still something that needs to be cleared up. I feel very tense when I look at the old boss.

Coach: Please stand facing the old boss and tell him, *"In the past I have often looked down on you and thought that I could do it better. But now I can acknowledge your life's work. You ran the business long before me and you trusted me. I respect that now."* Pay attention to whether or not these statements feel right as you say them.

When he has repeated the suggested statements, he seems relieved.

New boss: That was good! That's what was missing! Now the tension is easing up.

The old boss

In response, the *old boss* (position 6) says to the new one, *"I still have confidence in you.! If you get the employees involved, things will turn around again!"* Having said this, he looks intently at the new boss and reinforces his statement. *"Yes, that's right!"* The new boss welcomes this message. He feels accepted by the old boss and is able to relax in his position.

We have observed that the representative of the *employees* (position 3) has been showing signs of restlessness for some time now.

The employees

Coach: What is happening with the employees?

The representative of the employees indicates the new boss and declares vigorously, *"There are still some things to be cleared up here. It isn't that easy!"* We have the old boss and the employees stand facing the new boss.

Coach (turning to the old boss and pointing to the new boss): Tell him, and point to the employees as you say it, *"These people were my employees. They went through thick and thin with me. Please honour their efforts!"*

The representative of the old boss repeats these sentences.

Coach (turning to the new boss): Tell your employees, *"I'm sorry. I haven't respected your efforts enough. Now I can really see what you have done for the company."*

He repeats the suggested formulation and nods.

The statements also meet with agreement from the representative of the employees, who says, *"That fits for me and the tightness is letting go."* Only now is it possible for him to stand next to the new boss without resentment.

The last step of the constellation: The image of resolution

The old boss (position 6) is placed far to the left in the image of resolution. The *dismissed employees'* representative (position 7), after a number of different attempts to find a good place, finds that he feels best standing next to the old boss. At some distance we place the *new boss* (position 2), *Mr P* (position 1) and *the employees* (position 3). *The products* (position 5) are moved to a place where everyone can see them, and *the customers* (position 4) stand facing the boss and employees in a place where this representative can also see the products easily.

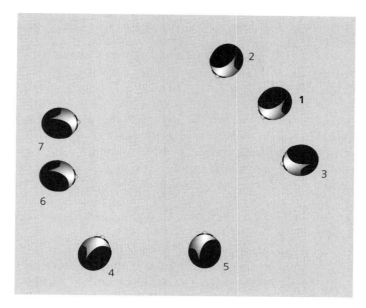

Fig. 5: image of resolution

When the old boss is given an appropriate place in the company system, his importance for the business is emphasised and can be acknowledged by the new boss. It is also confirmed that the previous employees still belong to the system and their efforts are recognised. As a result, the current employees can turn to the new boss and work cooperatively with him. The products come back into view and the customers begin to feel a renewed interest in the company and its products.

In this configuration, everyone feels motivated by the sight of the products waiting to be made and by their awareness of the customers of the company.

Mr P

Finally, we have Mr P take his representative's place in the constellation in the picture of resolution so that he can check it out for himself in relation to his initial issue.

Coach: Take your time to check out whether this order that we have found feels right to you.

Mr P: It looks all tidied up! (He grins.)

Coach: What do you mean by "tidied up?"

Mr P: Tidied up in the sense that from this place here (in the resolution configuration), I can see clearly and I have everybody within my field of vision. I like that!

Coach: Look at the representative of your customers. How does the relationship between the customers and the products seem to you?

Mr P: What I see here makes me feel optimistic.

Coach: Now look at the representative of the present employees. How do they seem? Are they going to stay or do they still want to leave?

Mr P: It looks like there's a lot of support there!

Mr P lets the image of resolution work on him a bit longer and then the coach ends the constellation.

The last step in a constellation is to release the representatives from their roles. Mr P thanks each representative for his help and calls each one by his real name. For example the product becomes Mr X again, the customers, Mr Y.

Feedback from representatives plays the major role in determining the direction of a constellation. Sentences of resolution such as those in the constellation dialogues have a relieving effect only when they are truly on the mark. This means that when representative experiences a sense of rightness with what is said, the relieving or resolving effects emerge.

A coach may often feel the effect of the suggested sentences directly. Sometimes however the effect can only be known through the reactions of the representatives. If a sentence is not on the mark, the coach lets it drop. In this way, constellation work is carried by the cooperative efforts of the coach and representatives.

In this case we found resolution for everyone involved in the constellation process. To conclude, we would like to point out the dynamics, the violation of systemic principles and possible practical applications of this final image.

The dynamics

When he took over the financial restructuring of the company, the new boss did not give his predecessor due recognition. He looked down on what the man had achieved and considered himself superior. The employees unconsciously wanted to "follow" their old boss and their colleagues who had been dismissed – that is, they wanted to leave the company out of loyalty to the others. As a result, their energy was capped and only partially available for the on-going work. The head of development had a strong sense of this missing energy. "*Somehow, they aren't really quite there.*" The customers missed the spirit of the company, which for them was connected to the old boss. They consequentially began to lose interest in the products. The products themselves, the basis of the business, were shunted aside, out of direct focus.

Violations of systemic principles
The balance between giving and taking was highly distorted when the new boss did not sufficiently recognise the achievements of the employees in terms of their commitment to the company. Under his leadership, the company demanded a lot but failed to reward with appropriate recompense or recognition.

The right to membership in the system was denied the old boss and the employees who had left. All members of a system, even those who have been fired or who have died, must be allowed to keep their place in the system and it is important to acknowledge their contribution to the business. In this case, that weighed particularly heavily since the employees who were dismissed had made a sacrifice that allowed the system to survive.

The hierarchy of the earlier over the later was not respected. Many employees had been in the company longer than the new boss. To gain their support he would have had to lead from the last position. In other words, he had to manage a balancing act in a split of hierarchies. In the ranking of the power structure he was on top, but in the sequence of seniority he was on the bottom, having arrived later than many of the employees.

Putting the solution into practice
Following the constellation we had a meeting with the managing director and the head of development about resolving the crisis and looking at what lessons were to be learned from the past. The director of development had already clearly regained confidence and energy. We advised the MD to rename the company and revert to the name of the founder. In addition we suggested that he heighten awareness of the founding father and his son, the previous boss, amongst the staff and customers. He agreed to do this and the

changes appeared in a new edition of the company brochure which included a picture of the founder of the company.

In the next phase, the employees formed project teams. Their efforts were now honoured and acknowledged. Interface teams working between development, production and sales went to work on the problems to be solved to improve quality. New practices catering to long-term relationships were initiated into customer service and customer satisfaction rose. Many of the old customers were wooed back. The high turnover in personnel also decreased.

3.2 "I CAN'T GET A FOOT IN HERE."
A YOUNG BUSINESS MANAGER IS NOT ACCEPTED BY HIS EMPLOYEES

Background information

A successful advertising agency was started by two partners twenty years ago. Partner A had the necessary customer contacts in industry, was well-informed about their needs and demands, and had a lot of business know-how. Partner B represented the creative, artistic side of the agency. With innovative ideas and vision, he helped the agency to flourish. After many years of working together successfully, partner A decided to leave the agency for personal reasons. Partner B regretted the loss of his partner, but was determined to keep the agency going on his own and took over the business side as well. He also felt an obligation to the employees since over the years about 50 people had been brought in and the agency now employed a staff of 65. A few of them gave notice following the departure of partner A, but most chose to continue working for the remaining partner. The financial situation of the well-run agency was stable, with many regular customers, and the business continued to run profitably. The working atmosphere also remained pleasant.

As the remaining partner, now working alone, gradually turned back to his interest in the creative, visionary aspects of the agency he hardly had time left for the business side of things, and the work atmosphere and financial situation changed. Regular customers began to drift away and as the business was now running in the red, a crisis committee was formed.

New business manager

The owner of the agency recognised that without the competence of his former partner, the business was not going to survive very long.

He decided to take in a manager to run the business side. He soon found a competent, dynamic, young businessman for the job. The new manager bent to his task with zeal, although the current condition of the books, organisational procedures, scheduling, and project development left him shaking his head in dismay. He began a thorough clean up and in short order he was able to achieve clarity and order in the organisation and the drain of old customers was halted. The employees stood behind him in gratitude that he had averted the crisis and secured their jobs.

The situation changed however when the young manager, sure of employee support, began to act as if he were solely responsible for the agency. He hardly even discussed his decisions with the original partner, his boss. The employees began to feel uneasy with these changes. True, there were now very clear organisational parameters, but they were no longer sure who their boss was and where their loyalties should lie. After all, the remaining original partner was still the owner and head of the firm, even though he was not involved in the running of the business. This was the way it felt to them and as a result, the new business manager could no longer get anywhere with them. Their resistance to him grew and his frustration and annoyance increased accordingly. Everything had started off so well! Health problems added to his misery as he suffered more and more frequently from stomach ailments. His popularity with employees and customers dropped to nil, and the crisis he had been hired to resolve arose again. Several major accounts were cancelled and competitors took advantage of the weakness of the company.

Systemically orientated intervention

The new business manager, Mr W, came to us for a consultation session. He was having great difficulty managing his employees. *"They are very resistant and some even boycott my decisions. I can't understand it! Initially, they were overjoyed that I had cleaned up that chaotic mess they were in."* He was looking for some tips and tools to re-establish a good working relationship with the employees but, according to his doctor, he also had to do something about the pressure he was under if he wanted to clear up his physical symptoms. Thorough medical tests and examinations had revealed no physical cause for the stomach problems he had been having for weeks and his doctor believed it was due to stress. It was certainly true that this man was under a lot of pressure at work, and he was not aware of any stress in other areas of his life.

We suggested to Mr W that the first step would be to use neutral representatives in a constellation to look at his professional situation. We explained to him that in this way we could possibly see more clearly where the stressful situation was originating, and what solution might be possible. He said that he actually only wanted to get rid of his stress-related symptoms and find a better way to handle his employees, but he was willing to try our way of working. We invited him to take part in a constellation seminar.

Just as a reminder, please remember that participants in a constellation seminar do not have access to the background information that you, the reader, are privy to. Representatives generally know only who or what they are supposed to represent. As constellation leaders, we need a minimum of information in order to "put wind in the sails of the constellation ship" and it normally consists solely of facts.

The next step: The constellation

Mr W (formulating his issue for the constellation): My goal is to find a way to win over the agency employees and customers again.
Coach: How would you recognise that our work had been successful and that you had achieved your aim?
Mr W: First of all, I wouldn't have any more stomach problems. Also, I would get back my enthusiasm for going in to work in the morning, because the employees would be "back in the boat". I'd be able to approach our customers in a more relaxed way and hopefully persuade them to come back again.

Mr W chooses representatives from the seminar participants and positions them according to his inner sense of how things are.

- *He, himself,* referred to in the constellation as "Mr W"
- *The remaining original partner and head of the agency,* called "the boss"
- *The employees,* represented by one person
- *The customers,* represented by one person
- *The competitors,* other advertising agencies, represented by one person

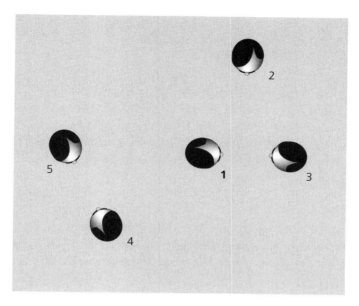

1	Business manager, Mr W	3	The employees
2	Owner and head of the agency (boss)	4	The customers
		5	The competitors

Fig. 1.: The situation as it is

We begin the round of feedback with the representative of *Mr W*.

Mr W

Mr W is standing facing the employees. The owner/boss stands off to one side. Behind Mr W are the customers and the competitors, facing each other.

Coach: How is Mr W's representative feeling?
Mr W: I feel weak and my knees are shaking. I keep staring, completely transfixed, at the employees. I can only see them. They seem very confrontational to me, as if they want something from me. I am aware of the customers back on one side. I don't know what's behind me and I'm not really interested. I can only see my boss out of the corner of my eye.
Coach: Are you aware of any sense of your boss that you could describe?

Mr. W: Yes, there's something like a lack of respect. The word "wimp" comes to mind. I feel rather superior to him.

The employees

Coach: How is the representative of the employees?

Employees: I'm just looking at him (Mr W) and I feel powerful and defiant. I can see the boss out of the corner of my eye. I feel sorry for him; he seems so needy. I can also see the customers out of the corner of my eye. I'd like to look more in that direction, but this other is stronger (pointing to Mr W).

The customers

Coach: What is the customers' representative aware of?

Customers: I am clearly focussed on the competition. There's a strong pull in that direction. I don't feel much about any of the others at the moment.

The competitors

Coach: What about the competitors? You seem to be doing well?

Competitors: I feel like a decoy, veeery attractive! I also seem to me to be very powerful and one thing is absolutely clear, my focus is there (indicates the customers)! The rest has nothing to do with me, and doesn't interest me either.

The boss

Coach: How are you doing?

Boss: Somehow, everything here is just passing me by. I'm also aware of something like resignation.

Coach: Where are you looking?

Boss: Somewhere off in the distance, right through the space between Mr W and the employees.

Coach: Is there anything else you notice?

Boss: Towards him (Mr W) I feel something like annoyance, or perhaps criticism. I feel some contact with the employees. That's very pleasant.

We ask Mr W, who has been observing from his seat, if he has any questions or anything to add.

Mr W: That's exactly how I experience the situation in the agency – completely muddled! I would really like to know which way my boss is looking! The fact that he isn't particularly interested in my conflict with the employees, well, that's also very close to reality!

The work in process – interim pictures
We begin by adding the original *partner who left* the agency to the constellation (position 6). Mr W chooses an additional representative for this role. He and the representative of the **boss** go through a short clearing process between the two of them, dealing with their relationship. It is only at this point that the remaining partner feels ready to really separate from his old partner. He now feels ready to look at the distribution of responsibility between him and Mr W and consider organising that differently. He becomes aware of the customers and the employees for the first time.

During the process work, the representative of Mr W becomes more aware of his presumptuous attitude towards the boss. After various steps, which we will not describe here, he is able to utter some resolving sentences in a way that they feel right to him and also get through to his boss. *"I have often felt superior to you and I had almost forgotten that you are the founder of the agency and my boss. I'm sorry."* These simple sentences have a positive effect and support the process of resolution. Afterwards, Mr W's representative is able to confront the employees and customers again with renewed strength and self-confidence.

Mr W and the *employees* also have some clearing to do and dialogue work helps them form a new basis for their work together. After various interventions they reach a realistic working relationship. The "helper syndrome" the employees were feeling towards their boss diminishes somewhat. We bring another representative into the picture to represent the *common task* (position 7) and the employees' need to rescue disappears completely. They can now relate to their boss as the boss, someone who sets clear goals for them. In the course of these clearing discussions, the customers feel a reciprocal pull back towards the agency and the competition loses some of its attractiveness. The representative of the competitors reacts with a desire to pull back somewhat.

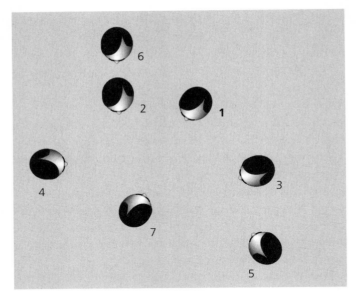

1	Business manager, Mr W	4	The customers
2	Owner and head of the	5	The competitors
	agency (boss)	6	The partner who left
3	The employees	7	The common task

Fig. 2: Picture of resolution

The image of resolution

The *partner who left* (position 6) is given a new place in the system. It turns out that the best place for him is to the right, supporting his former partner by "standing behind" him. In this way, the supportive effect of their good working relationship in the past is expressed symbolically during this building phase for the partner who has sole responsibility.

The boss (position 2) is visibly relieved and feels stronger when he consciously assents to his old partner leaving and draws on their history together as a good basis for the current tasks. In the final image of resolution he is particularly pleased that he can now see everyone and can be seen by all of them. When he makes eye contact with the representative of the common task, he feels challenged again. He remarks that he still feels some tendency to look off into the distance however. As this sometimes has systemic meaning, we check out the relationship to the work system again. No cause for this can be seen there, which means it may well be something that originates in his own family system.

For the *employees* (position 3), the feeling of power over Mr W has disappeared. They take their appropriate place next to him but prefer to keep some distance between them. From there, they are also in a position to see their boss as the boss instead of feeling pity for him. Looking at the common task increases their motivation.

The *customers* (position 4) feel as though they are once again respected and taken seriously by the agency. For their part, they feel willing to turn more energetically towards the agency. The attractiveness of the competitors has greatly diminished, but the customers still want to keep him in sight.

The *competitors'* (position 5) connection to the customers has weakened. The representative of the competitors pulls back somewhat, but still remains visible and present.

The *common task* (position 7) feels best near the customers, opposite the agency staff. There it waits rather impatiently for the "starting gun".

Mr W is surprised by how comfortable he feels now between his boss and the employees. The disdain he felt towards his boss has mellowed into a respectful attitude. He now feels acceptance from the employees instead of resistance, but he too needs to keep a bit of distance between them. *"Slowly send out a few feelers,"* he says. He is most pleased by a new sense of really belonging and he is aware of strength coming from the collective system, a support that will help him to move towards the customers and the common task. He does not feel a need to turn away when he looks at the competitors. *"Better to have them in sight than behind my back."*

Mr W now takes the place of his representative in the image of resolution, to feel the sense of it and check it against his initial issue.

Coach: How is this new place for you?
Mr W: It's unusual ,just' to stand in a row – not to have a prominent position any more. (after a pause) But it takes a load off me!
Coach: Now look at the employees again and think about your daily work together in the agency.

Mr W (Making eye contact with the representative of the employees): What is coming across from the employees is encouraging. If it stays that way this will work out.

Coach: Now make eye contact with the customers. (Mr W and the customers' representative look at each other and grin.)

Coach: So, what are the odds, Mr W?

Mr W: Not bad at all!

Coach: Good. We'll leave it like that!

With that, we end the constellation.

The dynamics

Great expectations for salvation were loaded on this young business manager, as he was supposed to lead the agency out of their crisis. He was in over his head but he accepted the task anyway, for reasons that probably could be traced to his own personality and his own family system. This would be an issue that he might explore later in a more personal setting if the need arises. The boss/owner of the business had not really integrated the separation from his former business partner. When he was able to take that step in the constellation, he could let go and was again ready to fully engage in the business. His energy, however was still partially elsewhere, which is why he repeatedly drifted away from the concrete situation into the distance. Since this is an issue that probably stems from his own family system, like Mr W, he can explore that later in a personal setting, for example in a family constellation.

The results of this constellation show clearly what kind of dead end might await us if we, as consultants, too hastily follow a client's wishes for training. Leadership training and stress management seminars are valuable aids, but in this case they would not have touched the fundamental problem.

Violations of systemic principles

The new business manager, Mr W, stepped into a position of power that he was not entitled to. Because he was the newest in the company, he had to lead from the last place. In his presumption, he violated the position of the head of the company (the boss) in the basic hierarchy, and also the hierarchical priority of the earlier over the later (employees). The employees became confused about their roles and the position of their boss (*"You have to feel sorry for him"*). In relationship to Mr W, they assumed an inappropriate role by not recognising his leadership role.

To continue the process, we offer coaching to the owner/boss and the young business manager to clarify their contributions to the situation. This would be useful for the young manager so that he can avoid falling into the same kind of traps in the future as he did in this case. To complete the process, we offer coaching for the two of them to clarify their conflicts and work out some guidelines for their future work together. Once clear lines of communication were re-established, the agency prospered again and Mr W's physical symptoms were greatly diminished.

3.3 "WHAT DO WE NEED IN ORDER TO GROW TOGETHER?"
PROBLEMS FOLLOWING A GERMAN-FRENCH COMPANY MERGER

Background information

In a large German company in the consumer goods industry, business was good for many years and the time came to think about expanding. The firm had already bought a series of smaller German competitors in the field, but the most important rival was a French company. After a long period of negotiation, they were also able to take over this competitor. The new, larger company was run under the German name with the French name mentioned only in an add-on.

"Nothing will change for you! Your jobs will still be there for you," the head of the company assured the workers, particularly the French employees. The German management wanted to get back to the normal everyday business as soon as possible and the figures seemed to support that move. The market reacted positively and company shares increased in value.

IT problems

In one area, however, there were soon enormous difficulties. The whole IT system was to be standardised and management expected the French employees to follow the German guidelines and procedures. *"No problem,"* replied the French managers, *"of course we will work together with you on this."*

A team of German IT experts travelled to France to get their French colleagues started on the project, and they judged the initial meetings of the two teams positively. The French were friendly but non-committal. The Germans, who were not familiar with the French cultural mentality, interpreted the lack of objections or argument to their suggestions as agreement. A few days later, however, when it came to putting it into practice, the bomb dropped suddenly in a meeting when the French IT staff flatly refused to accept the German system. It was simply impossible, they maintained, because the German structures were in no way compatible with the procedures of the French affiliate. Complete bewilderment on the part of the Germans! *"But you all agreed! We had sorted it all out! What on earth is the matter?"* The French countered, *"It can't possibly work that way."* The German system was deemed too inflexible and would not do justice to their particular needs.

Management did not react with understanding, but tried to push the project through with pressure, sanctions, and orders. They did not meet with open resistance from the French, but there was a never-ending stream of arguments that continuously disrupted and impaired the work. Slowly the head of the German company began to see that the conflict could not be dealt with their way, and we were brought in as consultants.

Systemically orientated intervention

We had our first meeting with one of the German directors, Dr B. In answer to our question as to where he saw the problem, he just shook his head. *"That's why we have come to you. As we see it, we have done everything that had to be done. For example, we did an intensive retraining with the French staff to help them work into the German IT system. So, from our side, everything has been taken care of. Nonetheless, there is a tough core of resistance that we just can't explain."* To clarify the background of the problem, we suggested a constellation of the organisation as a first step, using neutral representatives who were not involved with the company. He was not familiar with the constellation method, but was willing to try something new. The deciding factor for him was the *relatively low expenditure of time and money* as compared to other methods.

The constellation

Dr B formulates his issue for the constellation; *"My aim is a good working relationship, free of tension, between the French and German employees. I would also like to understand exactly what this conflict is about."* When we have gathered enough information for a constellation, Dr B chooses representatives from the seminar participants and places them according to his inner sense.

- *He, himself,* referred to as Dr B
- *The French employees,* represented by one person
- *The German employees,* represented by one person
- *The original French company*
- *The common task*

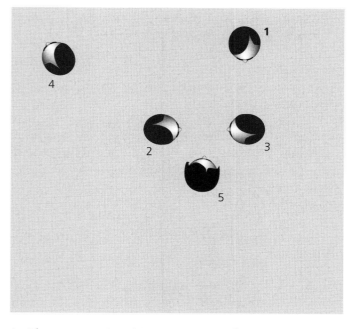

1 The representative of Dr B, member of the board of directors of the new merged firm	3 The German employees
	4 The original French company
2 The French employees	5 Their common task

Fig. 1: The situation as it is

When the representatives have had time to feel their way into their roles and their positions, we begin with the first round of feedback.

Dr B

Dr B is looking at the German employees, who are facing and looking at the French employees. The common task is standing a short distance away, between the French and German employees. The original French company is far off to the right, facing away from the system.

Coach: How is Dr B's representative feeling?
Dr B: I am aware of the German employees and the common task. I feel something like impatience and annoyance towards the French employees. The common task is not looking at me, but she should be! I hardly notice whatever is standing off to my right (the original French company). I've actually forgotten who that representative is!

The French employees

The representative of the French employees is standing directly opposite the German employees.

Coach: How are you doing? You're not standing very comfortably!
French Employees: I'm standing here totally twisted up, completely mixed up and turned around. I feel a tendency to turn to the left. It's a very strong impulse.
Coach: Go with it.

(He turns so far to the left that he is facing Dr B's representative. He nods in affirmation).

French Employees: Yes, that feels right. There's something here to be clarified. I feel extremely angry when I look at him (indicating the representative of Dr B)

When we ask the representative to express this feeling with some gesture or a statement, he hesitates. Glancing sideways at Dr B, who is sitting outside the constellation following the proceedings, the representative of the French employees says apologetically, *"This could get rough!"*

80

We encourage him to express what he is feeling in this role of the French employees. After a time, his body posture changes and he blurts out in a tone of contempt, *"You can stuff it!"* Afterwards, he exhales audibly.

Coach: Aha! That's where we are!

Dr B's representative seems very affected by this outburst. After a while the coach asks the representative of the French employees if he has anything more to say.

French Employees: I can feel someone standing diagonally behind me (the original French company). There's something heavy, serious there. I also experience the common task as very pushy, as if she wants to get in between my colleagues and me.

The German employees
Coach: How is the representative of the German employees? How did you feel before, and how do you feel now that the representative of the French employees has turned away from you?
German Employees: At the beginning, when we were standing opposite each other (indicated the representative of the French employees), I was very uncomfortable. I felt some criticism towards me but I was thinking, "Boy, you've got the wrong person!" As he turned away, I felt very relieved. From my right (Dr B) I feel support, but I also feel critical of him. The common task seems to me to be too pushy, too close. I don't feel anything at all towards the representative who is facing away.

The original French company
The representative of the original French company is standing with his head hanging down, far away from the group and facing away from them.

Coach: How are you doing, so far away from everybody?
Original French company: I feel like a lost cause out here. Somehow disheartened, resigned.
Coach: Do you have any urge to move in some way?

Original French company: Yes, I would like to turn around!
Coach: Good, we'll come back to that in a moment.

The common task

The representative of the common task is standing at a short distance from the German and French employees, somewhat between them.

Coach: How are you feeling, as representative of the common task?
Common Task: This is not a good place for me. I can't make eye contact with anyone and I have to make a real effort to even see anybody out of the corner of my eye. This is much too close for me. I feel like I want to move backwards.
Coach: Go with that movement, please.
The representative of the common task draws back several steps. Exhaling, she says, *"I can breathe now."*

Dr B

We address Dr B who is watching from his place.

Coach: What do you have to say to this?
Dr B: I feel very affected and concerned by what I see here. I'm still not clear, though, about the reason for these feelings of the French employees.
Coach: If you look at where you placed the representative of the original French company and remember what he said, we could possibly assume that the conflict in the company, seen systemically, has to do with neglecting to give due recognition. Something like that has effects on a company.

Next, we proceed to work with the process in the constellation.

The work in process – interim pictures

First of all we ask the representative of the original French company to turn around so he can see the others (in the first configuration he was standing with his back to everyone else). He seems relieved. One at a time, Dr B, the French employees, and the German employees are placed opposite the original French company. They each speak sentences of acknowledgement. For example, Dr B says, *"Without you, our company would not be what it is today."* Bowing to the original French company also supports the process of resolution, relieving some of the burden. The German and French employees honour the French company in a similar way.

In the course of the process work, feedback from Dr B makes clear how little attention was paid to the needs of the French employees after the merger. At this point there is a long clearing process on this issue. Only after this clearing is it possible for the French employees to take in and believe the sentences of resolution from Dr B, such as, *"I'm sorry. We have overlooked you and your needs, but this is going to change."*

The French employees stand opposite the German employees. Following the previous process work, they both find it easy to look at their colleagues with good will. The representative of the French tells his German colleague, *"We have nothing against you. If you could just come a step or two in our direction, we could make a good team!"*

The German employees are brought face to face with Dr B. Although their accusatory attitude towards him has weakened, the representative of the German employees feels compelled to verbalise his main criticism. *"You have left us in the lurch! From a position of leadership you could have helped to integrate the French workers, but you unloaded the problem on to us!"* Having said this, his anger subsides and his is ready to listen to Dr B, who assures him, *"I'm sorry. I can see where we were negligent. This is our responsibility."*

Finally, the German and French employees stand before the common task. The representative of the common task seems quite agitated. *"I've stood in the background long enough. Now I want a place where I belong."* The German and French employees confirm that they can now take on the challenge of their common task together.

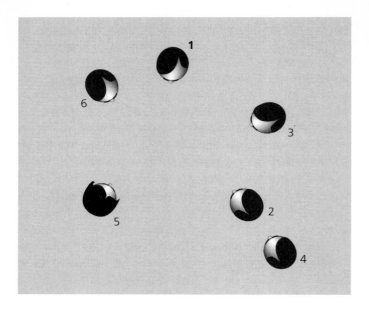

1	The representative of Dr B,	3	The German employees
	member of the board of	4	The original French company
	directors of the new merged firm	5	Their common task
2	The French employees	6	The new post-merger company

Fig. 2: Picture of resolution

The image of resolution

For *Dr B* (position 1), it is important to be in a position where he has an overview of everything. He feels a sense of "emptiness" on his right side, as if something were missing there. When we add a representative for the *new post-merger company* (position 6) in this place, he says, *"That was missing!"*

The *German employees* (position 3) find a good position to the left of Dr B, but there is a certain distance between them.

The *French employees* (position 2) stand to the left of the German employees. They are in position to have good contact with their German colleagues, to Dr B, and to the entire company. It is important for them to have the original French company behind them for support.

The representative of the *original French company* (position 4) comments, *"I am doing well now. I feel a need to pull back a bit. I feel well cared for in the new company."* But for the representative of the French employees the nearness of the original French company is still important. It seems as though having had their needs ignored has left such a deep wound that they cannot yet trust the new management, and still want the original company backing them up.

For the representative of the *common task* (position 5) it is not difficult to find the right place. For her it is of primary importance to be able to see and be seen by everyone.

Finally, we invite Dr B to take the place of his representative in the picture of resolution, to get the feeling of it and check it against his presenting issues. He looks round the circle of the constellation. He can very clearly feel support from the new company on his right side. He looks long and hard at the French employees, the constant "thorn in the side". Dr B shakes his head sceptically: *"I can hardly believe it. The representative looks quite peaceful! I'm going to be curious to see what happens in practice."*

Noticing his scepticism, we offer Dr B the opportunity to better understand the process his representative has experienced.

It can happen that representatives progress more quickly in the process of resolution than the person they are representing. They have more freedom because they are not connected to the issue.

Coach: You seem sceptical. If you are willing, we will add one more step. (Dr B agrees).

We ask him to stand facing the French employees himself and say to them, *"I'm sorry about what has happened. I will give you my support in the future."*

Coach: Does that seem right for you?
Mr B: It's a relief!

His message also comes across to the French employees. In the next step Dr B stands opposite the original French company and again speaks the sentence of resolution himself. *"Without your company we would not be what we are today."* He then bows in respect to the original French company, and then returns to his own position in the constellation.

The new company then repeats the same words to the French employees and the original French company and strengthens the message by bowing respectfully.

Dr B seems more relaxed. When asked if he has anything more to add, he says, *"That was an important step."* When Dr B has released the representatives from their roles, we end the constellation.

The dynamics

In their focus on the expansion of the whole company, the management of the concern had almost lost sight of the basis for the growth spurt, which was taking over the French company and its employees. They were taken into consideration only as economic factors in the larger planning. The French felt over-run and reacted with resistance. Dr B, as the representative of the board of directors, had unconsciously unloaded the conflict on to his employees to solve. In the first configuration, he placed the French and German employees opposite each other, which in a constellation may express confrontation. The representative of the French employees however felt very clearly (*I feel mixed up and turned around*) that the conflict had to be solved elsewhere.

Violations of systemic principles

When the firm changed names, the French company's right to its own identity and history was ignored and, consequently, the rights of the employees to belong to their company and to keep their nationality. Unintentionally but unavoidably the Germans, particularly the IT specialists working on their project in France, violated the systemic order of the priority of the those who came first (the French) over those who came later.

Implementing the solution in practice

The name of the French company now appears in the logo of the firm, in second place. In this way the smaller partner is recognised. The French again have control over their internal procedures. Interestingly enough, after a period of time it turned out that it was possible after all to switch over to the German IT system without any difficulty. To smooth the merger process, a series of training programmes were begun, in team building and communication, which in addition to a practical training programme, include an opportunity for the Germans and the French to learn about and better understand each other's culture. Special coaching was planned for the directors and management to practice intercultural relationship management.

It is particularly important in mergers to pay attention to the sensibilities of the smaller partner. Otherwise, in conflict situations both sides tend to see only the negative side of the opposition.

In intercultural relationship management, both sides are learning to broaden their vision. Here, a "development square" is helpful for identifying imbalances and rectifying them. In Chapter 5 you will see how that functions.

3.4 "I WANT THE REWARDS WE HAVE EARNED." RED INK IN A BRANCH PURCHASED BY A MEDIUM-SIZED FAMILY BUSINESS

Background information

In a medium-sized family business operating worldwide, two of the three branches (A and B) were operating profitably. The third (C), despite fine products and a favourable market situation, continually operated in the red. The business managers of A and B were not enthusiastic about the prospect of sacrificing their profit long term for the survival of the weak branch.

The situation was especially explosive because the three managers were brothers. When their father, the founder of the company, retired they took over the three branches so that each one could manage their own area. They had little contact with each other privately. In business meetings, criticism rained down on the youngest brother who was responsible for the deficit-producing branch. Together the three of them had hired a business consultant to solve the problem of branch C.

Restructuring an area operating at a deficit

The consultant produced various analyses and studies on the economic and organisational roots of the problem and recommended restructuring measures. All three managers agreed with the analyses and the suggested measures. With the help of the consultant they reconceptualised this area, reorganised, altered hierarchies and strengthened sales. The employees and management team in the C branch shared the optimism of the three directors and went to work with new enthusiasm.

Everything started off well, but success remained elusive and the customers continued to show little interest. One peculiar aspect was that all three brothers more or less shrugged their shoulders and went back to business as usual, even though they could see that the C branch, even with this comprehensive business consultation, continued to ail. The idea of eliminating branch C altogether was discarded because the youngest brother would then have no area of his own to supervise and their now-dead father had expressly wanted the company to continue under the leadership of his three sons.

Through a personal contact with the youngest of the brothers, we were asked to advise the company systemically. The contact arose in the context of a seminar on family constellations which the youngest brother, Mr S, took part in. In the family constellation it was clear that he unconsciously represented a family member who was poorly regarded and then simply forgotten about. This person was accused, without proof, of having treated his children unfairly, and had been excluded from the family.

In family entanglements you can often see that the excluded person is later "represented" by someone else in the family system. What that means is that the "representative" unconsciously acts to show solidarity with the excluded person either by suffering himself or trying to make reparations.

The family constellation had a good effect on Mr S and he was able to change his inner orientation and present himself with more self-confidence. Because of his personal experience, which had been helpful to him, he was interested in looking at the situation in the business systemically using a constellation. His older brothers agreed to the procedure, but laughed it off as one more attempt that would lead to nothing.

Systemically orientated intervention

In a meeting with Mr S we gather the necessary information about the company system:

- Who founded the firm and when?
- When was each branch added?
- Have there been waves of employees quitting or dismissals?
- Is there any person or area that is poorly regarded, or that has been forgotten?

Everything sounded very harmonious. The branch that he directs (branch C) has belonged to the company for a long time. It was purchased by his father and ran smoothly at the beginning, but began to fail after the war. Even when the other branches experienced an upward spurt, this one did not recover. When we ask for more details of the acquisition of this branch, it turns out that the problematic part of the firm goes back to a company that his father got in the 30's from Jewish owners. In the course of "Aryanisation", the Nazis forced the Jewish family to sell their business well below its actual value. The former Jewish owners were never heard of again. No one gave this much thought later, since the business was properly run, and all the employees had been kept on. As Mr S reports this he becomes very thoughtful.

The constellation

The systemic constellation is done in an open seminar using neutral representatives with no connection to the company.

Mr S formulates his issue: *"The company branch C is doing poorly for no identifiable reason. My goal is to finally have some success with our fine products. It is also important to me to find out what is behind this situation."*

We ask Mr S to choose representatives from the seminar participants and place them according to his inner sense of things:

- *He, himself:* Managing director of branch C, referred to in the constellation as Mr S.
- *His father:* Now deceased, founder of the firm
- *The eldest brother:* Managing director of branch A
- *The middle brother:* Managing director of branch B
- *Branch C* of the company
- *The market*
- *The customers*, one representative for all customers

Mr S is standing turned away from all the others, near Branch C. Both are looking out of the system into the distance. His two brother stand at some distance from him next to each other, looking in the direction of the representative of the market and customers, who are also placed parallel to one another and are looking at the two brothers. The deceased founder of the company stands directly behind his two eldest sons.

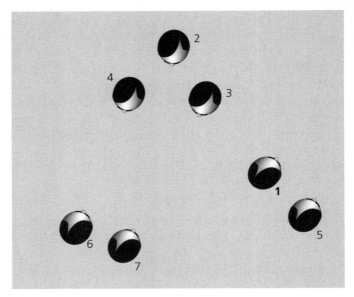

1	Mr S, managing director of branch C	4	The middle brother and managing director of branch B
2	The father and founder of the firm	5	Branch C
3	The eldest brother and managing director of branch A	6	The market for the products of this company
		7	The customers

Fig. 1: Situation as it is

Mr S

Coach: How is Mr S's representative feeling?

Mr S: I feel weak, beaten down and my shoulders are slumped together. Besides that I feel compelled to keep looking at one spot. I can only see the C branch out of the corner of my eye. I don't feel much of a connection to him. He seems very weak to me. There's another feeling though that's difficult to describe – something like guilt. Yes, in that direction.

Coach: Can you describe this guilt any more concretely?

Mr S: I feel it when I look at branch C.

Coach: What do you notice about your relationship to the others?

Mr S: Mainly I'm interested in this direction (indicates the point where he is looking). What's happening behind me has very little importance to me.

Branch C

Coach: How is the representative of branch C? You look as if you can hardly stand up.

Branch C: That's true. I feel like a balloon that the air has been let out of, weak and with no energy. I keep looking at the same spot as Mr S.

Coach: Are you aware of anything else?

Branch C: The market and the customers must be standing someplace, but I can't feel anything from them. The brothers and their father are standing somewhere off to my side. He (indicates Mr S standing next to him) has almost no effect on me. I don't feel any sense of connection to him.

Coach: Do you feel any urge to move?

Branch C: Yes, I feel pulled down.

Coach: Go with that feeling.

(The representative of branch C drops slowly down to his heels, his arms stretched out in front of him, his head between his shoulders and murmurs, *"Not exactly comfortable, but it feels right."*)

Father and founder of the firm

The father, founder of the firm, is standing a short distance behind and between the first and second sons.

Coach: How are you doing? You look rather pleased.

Father: I hardly dare to say so with all this drama all around me, but I feel extraordinarily fine! My two sons here in front of me …I'm so proud of them! Also the market and the customers are looking at all three of us with interest. When I look over there though … (indicates the direction of Mr S and branch C), I feel somewhat defensive. I don't want to see that at all.

The eldest brother

The eldest brother is placed to the left of his younger brother with his father diagonally behind him. He is looking at the customers and the market.

Coach: How is the eldest brother's representative?

Eldest brother: I don't feel particularly content in this place. I feel torn. On the one hand I am looking at the market and the customers and that's good. But I can't fully concentrate on that because I feel so strongly drawn in the direction of my youngest brother. Yeah, that's the right description, I feel pulled apart! I feel a strong need to help him. I'm not pleased at all about having my father behind me. I want to see him. I don't feel much of a connection to my middle brother.

The middle brother

The middle brother stands at a short distance to the right of his elder brother. He is looking at the customers and the market.

Coach: How are you doing?
Middle brother: It's not easy to describe. I feel very big and powerful. I can feel my father (indicates representative behind him) behind me. I have good contact with the market and the customers. I can be sure of them! I have hardly any connection to my elder brother. When I look in the direction of my younger brother and the C branch however, I feel something like contempt. The word "failure" occurs to me.

The market and the customers

Coach: How are the representatives of the market and the customers doing?
Market: I'm doing fine. Over there, where I'm looking (indicates the group of two brothers and their father) I feel a lot of strength. I can't feel anything from Mr S and C branch. I like having the customers here on my right side.
Customers: I feel very much the same as the market. This is a good place here! What's going on over to my right doesn't interest me. Here's where the action is! (He indicates the direction of the two brothers and their father.)

After the first round of feedback, we turn to Mr S, who has been watching the constellation from his seat.

Coach: Have you got any idea where the two of them are looking?
Mr S: I don't know. I have no idea. But, I feel very affected by what I am seeing. At the moment, I can't say any more than that.

Work in process – interim pictures

We begin the process work at this point.

The next step is to have Mr S choose another representative from the seminar participants and to place him where the two representatives (Mr S and branch C) having been looking the whole time. Now we check this out.

Coach: (indicating the newly placed representative) He is representing the Jewish former owner of the company that was bought (and later became branch C).

The representative of Mr S feels an irresistible urge to move closer to this representative. The representative of the Jewish owner looks at him very seriously.

Coach: (to Mr S's representative) Please look at him and say to him, "I bow to your fate." If you can really do it, actually bow down to him. (The representative speaks this sentence and bows deeply.)

The father and his two other sons seem to be very affected by this. They also feel a need to bow down to the Jewish owner. After this initial expression of respect for this terrible fate, we place the father and his three sons in front of the representative of the Jewish owner and have him say, *"These are my three sons. They are carrying on my life's work. This is my youngest son. He is carrying on your life's work in our company.* (indicating the C branch) *Please agree to this!"*
    The representative of the Jewish owner looks over to the branch C representative, who has slowly straightened up during the process of the work. He then looks round the circle and nods. The sense of empathy in the room is palpable and people appear to be very touched. There is a long, silent pause.
    We place Mr S facing branch C. He states emphatically, *"Now things can move forward. I'm ready!"* They both move spontaneously towards each other and shake hands.

Coach: (to Mr S) Look at branch C again and tell him, "We had a very fateful start, but now let's look towards the future together."

He repeats these words, which immediately have an effect on the customers and the market as well. These representatives look at Mr S and branch C with interest for the first time.

Finally, Mr S and branch C stand in front of the father and the other two brothers. We ask Mr S to say, *"Now I have the strength to follow a course that will lead to success. Together with these two* (indicates the customers and the market) *branch C will finally get the rewards it has earned."*

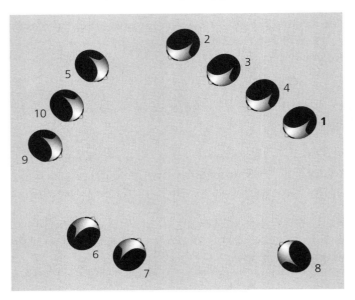

1	Mr S, Managing director of branch C	5	Branch C
2	The father and founder of the firm	6	The market for the products of this company
3	The eldest brother and managing director of branch A	7	The customers
		8	The Jewish owner
4	The middle brother and managing director of branch B	9	Branch A
		10	Branch B

Fig. 2: The last step of the constellation, the image of resolution

Mr S (position 1) stands as the youngest in the row of three siblings. In this position he feels strength from his two brothers at his side that supports him in action. It is important for him to keep the market and the customers in sight and they are looking at him with interest. He is pleased to see branch C standing as an equal next to branch A and branch B (which we have added to the final configuration of resolution).

The father (position 2), as founder of the firm and head of the family, is given a position to the far right in the resolution picture. This place feels right to him, but he would prefer to be standing supportively behind his youngest son. The youngest son shakes his head, no. We ask the father to accept this, for him, "second-best" place. The clearing at the level of the family relationships can be continued in a different context.

The eldest brother (position 3) has the position that he is entitled to as the eldest – to the right in the row of siblings. He experiences more strength than previously. In the first configuration, Mr S had placed him between the middle and youngest brother, that is, in second place in the order of siblings. In our experience, a placement that is not in accord with the systemic principles usually weakens the one involved. For this brother it is particularly important to keep sight of the Jewish owner. He remarks, *"When I look at him, I don't feel as much need to help my youngest brother. Also, that feeling of being torn apart is gone. It's okay like this."*

The middle brother (position 4) takes the position in the row of siblings that belongs to him – the middle. For him this feels unusual at first. *"My sense of being powerful has disappeared. I've shrunk a bit, but it's somehow a healthy shrinking. My feeling of contempt towards my younger brother is gone. What's particularly important is that despite being "shrunk", I still have contact with the market and the customers.*

The representative of *branch C* (position 5) now stands as an equal next to *branch A* (position 9) and *B* (position 10), which we have added to the picture of resolution. He is also able to stand straight and strong. It is particularly important for him to have eye contact with the customers and the market, who now look at him with interest.

The representatives of the *market* (position 6) and the *customers* (position 7) are standing sided by side, visible to everyone else.

The Jewish owner (position 8) has been given a place in the system of the company where everyone can see him.

At the end, we invite Mr S to take his representative's place in the constellation's image of resolution, to experience the effects and notice the connections to his initial issue. After a while he exhales audibly and looks at each person in the constellation, spending a long time looking at the representative of the Jewish owner. He then says, *"My thanks to all of you. I never would have suspected that the problem lay in this direction."*

Coach: How are the customers and the market looking at you?

Mr S (looking again at the representatives of the customers and the market): Yes, they are aware of me. I get the feeling that I have something they need and they have something I need. We are equals. That's a good basis for a business relationship! (The representatives of the customers and the market both nod.)

We end the constellation with the release of the representatives from their roles.

The dynamics

In the family system, the youngest brother, as manager of the company previously owned by Jews (now branch C), represented the forgotten Jewish family who had been forced out of their business. As if to recall the injustice they had been subjected to, his section of the business ran at a loss. When the original owner was honoured in his difficult fate and given an appropriate place in the system, Mr S felt supported and could look forward to the future.

Since this case involves a family business, tensions from the family system have particularly strong effects on the company system.

Violations of systemic principles

The right of the Jewish founding family to belong to the system was not respected. They were simply forgotten. That gave the injustice done to them and their personal fate a particular weight in the system of the current company, which had effects on branch C and contributed to its failure to prosper. At the same time, the right of priority for those who came first (the first owners) over those who came later (the successive owners) was not respected. The balance of giving and taking was gravely violated by the forced sale of the original company at less than its true value.

Implementation of the solution in practice

The most important step here is the symbolic honouring of the Jewish family. Their name and their story are to be documented in the foyer of the company building. The company decided to make a donation to a fund for the still surviving victims of the Jewish persecution and to participate in the compensatory fund established by German businesses for those who had to work as forced labour under the Nazi regime.

To improve their communication, the three managers partici-
pated in a coaching process. Although it is still too soon to evaluate
the full effects of this systemic consultation, six months after the first
intervention, new contracts for branch C have increased.

3.5 "WHO IS THE UNDERCOVER BOSS HERE?"
A BUSINESS CONSULTANT ON THE WRONG TRACK

Background information

A successful business consultant was hired by the directors of a bank
to advise them on the issue of succession. Besides the chairman of
the board, who had run the business of the bank for 20 years, there
were three additional members of the board. The chairman planned
to retire in two years' time. When he and the consultant had weighed
the pros and cons of each candidate, in-house and external, he decided to name one of the three directors as his replacement. During
the transition phase, the consultant was to support the board of directors with coaching. She spoke at length to each of the directors,
learning about their hopes, plans, goals and concerns.

She was able to establish a good working climate with open communication and could help build a bond of trust between the retiring
chairman and his successor. The old chairman made it clear that,
having made his decision, he no longer regarded himself as the boss,
but rather "primus inter pares", the first among equals, and he
wished to work with the directors' team. This surprised the consultant, and also the successor to the chair and the other directors, since
the old boss had always exercised a rather traditional leadership
style. Shortly thereafter, the old boss and the new boss began to
handle the bank business together on an equal basis. As the transition continued, the old boss began to pull out of the day-to-day business and merely supervised his successor's decisions.

At this point something completely inexplicable developed. The
more power and decision-making the successor took over, the more
conspicuously his behaviour as boss changed. Always a model of
precision and dependability, he now nonchalantly postponed ap-
pointments with customers at the last minute, or cancelled them altogether. He often came late to meetings and reduced his presence in
the office to a minimum. The old boss could not explain this change

of character. Many meetings followed between the old boss, the new boss and the consultant, who moderated the process and invested a lot personally to ensure its success.

She most insistently made clear to the incoming chairman what the consequences of his behaviour could be, and she supported the old boss in his plea to the younger man not to risk everything in this way. In individual sessions the old boss confided to the consultant that he had serious concerns about what was happening. It was now too late to find someone else to take his place because he was going to leave the bank at the time he had set, and by that time everything had to be running smoothly. The consultant was to do whatever she could to help his designated successor find his way back to his trustworthy, dependable self. Everything was depending on it!

Task of the consultant

For the consultant, there was a lot at stake and she really had to get the transfer of power back on track. If the process went completely off the rails, she would not be able to fulfil her contract and, among other unpleasant consequences, her reputation as a competent consultant would be endangered. She continued to hold almost daily meetings with the old boss and the new director and tried to understand and motivate the new man. However, the more effort she put in and the more she worried about the business, the more casually the successor treated his tasks and the more condescending he was towards her. *"You're much too uptight about all this! Relax!"*, was his reaction.

At this point it became clear to her that things could not continue in this way, as she was getting completely bogged down. When another consultant told her about systemic coaching, she turned to us with a request for supervision.

Systemically orientated intervention

The consultant, Ms M, describes the situation from her viewpoint. It seems clear to her that it is not just a matter of the successor to the top job basking in his new position of power, but there has also been a shift of power in his personality. She cannot see the reason behind this. She would like to know from us what she could do to get out of this dead end and successfully complete her job. At this moment she would be perfectly happy to just throw in the towel.

She agrees with our evaluation that there is little sense in continuing to focus on the successor until the fundamental dynamics become clearer, including his role in the business system and her own. We agree to set up the situation in a systemic constellation in a neutral setting with non-involved representatives.

The constellation

When we have gathered the necessary information for the constellation, we assist Ms M to formulate her issue as precisely as possible. The consultant's formulation is this: *"I want to know what went wrong and what I can do to fulfil my obligations successfully."*

Ms M chooses representatives from the group of participants and places them according to her inner sense.

- *She, herself*, referred to in the constellation as Ms M, or the "consultant"
- *The old boss*, the chairman of the board who is about to retire from the bank
- *The new boss*, a member of the board of directors, successor to the chair
- *Director A*
- *Director B*
- *The customers of the bank*, with one representative for all the customers

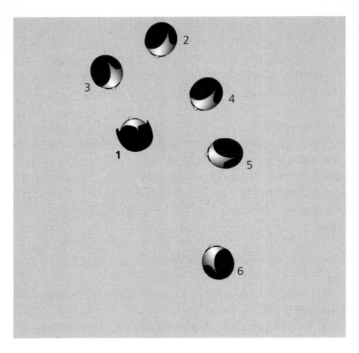

1	The business consultant, Ms M	4	Director A
2	The old boss	5	Director B
3	The new boss	6	The bank's customers

Fig. 1: The situation as it is

Before we begin the round of feedback, we send up a "trial balloon".

Coach: If you look at this configuration, who do you think the "undercover" boss is? (At first the representatives look at the coach in confusion. After a while their eyes turn to the consultant.)

Then we begin asking the representatives for feedback, beginning with the representative of Ms M.

Ms M

With the exception of the bank customers, all the representatives are facing Ms M at a close distance.

Coach: How is the representative of Ms M feeling? Everyone is looking at you!

Ms M: Awful, absolutely awful! I am so tense! "Undercover boss", well, yes, there's something to that. Everyone except the new head is looking at me full of expectation. He seems to me to be defiant. I'm much too hemmed in here. I need to move backwards, but at the same time I feel rooted to the ground.

Coach: Who are you looking at?

Ms M: My eye is drawn to the new boss. I would like to go over and shake him to make him stop looking at me that way. I feel helpless against him, but at the same time there's a sense of superiority. Strange combination!

Coach: If we didn't know that this is a business relationship, one might think this had to do with a family scene – a mother trying to raise her rebellious son! (Both nod.)

The old boss

The old boss is standing in the middle, behind the new boss and Director A. He is looking at Ms M.

Coach: How is the representative of the old boss doing?

Old boss: I have no strength. I can only look at the consultant. Forward, off to the left, I am not aware of much (Director A and B are standing there). When I look to the right (to the new boss) I feel angry. I'm hardly aware of the customers of the bank.

The new boss

Coach: How are you feeling?

New boss: Powerful and rebellious! Particularly when I look at the consultant. There's also a feeling something like "Hey, bring it on! I'm cool!" Yeah, something sort of casual. But one thing is clear; I don't take orders from this woman! In her direction I've got all my defences up. I miss the old boss, who I can only see out of the corner of my eye. I would have liked to have him next to me. I hardly feel any contact to the other directors. I can see the bank customers, but my attention is all in this direction (indicated the representative of Ms M).

Director A

Director A is standing next to the new boss, but at some distance.

Coach: What is happening with the representative of Director A?

Director A: To my left it's just neutral (towards Director B). I can't see the customers. I am clearly looking towards the consultant. As far as I'm concerned, she could come closer. We need her urgently! To the right, towards the new boss, I experience a feeling of mistrust and anger. I am not happy at all that the old boss is so far back.

Director B

The representative of Director B is to the left of Director A and is looking in the direction of Ms M.

Director B: He (indicating Director A) has already said everything important. I feel exactly the same way!

The bank's customers

The representative of the bank's customers is standing far back in the configuration, looking at the scene. He has been noticeably restless for some time, shifting his weight from one foot to the other and looks quite sullen.

Coach: How is it going with the bank's customers?
Bank's customers: I am completely out in the cold here! True, I can sort of see everyone, but no one is paying any attention to me! I feel totally superfluous. If this goes on any longer, I'm out of here!

At this point we turn to Ms M, who has been following the constellation from her seat.

Ms M: I was a bit taken aback myself that I put my representative so near to my client. The rebellious behaviour of the new boss towards me, and my representative's reaction to it sound very familiar to me. The comment about the "family scene" really gave me something to think about, especially the fact that both the representatives nodded. I would like to find out more about that, also just for myself, in terms of my work as a consultant.
Coach: It looks as though you both (indicates Ms M and the new boss) have unconsciously mixed something up in your work relationship that does not belong there. What that is, exactly, we could only guess at this point. Let's wait for the constellation.

Although the representative of Ms M wanted more space between her and the others, she admitted that her feet were "rooted to" the floor. Clarifying her relationship to the old boss, the new boss, and the board of directors allows this rigidity to dissolve. To symbolically give back whatever had been taken over that was too much, we have Ms M actually hand the new boss an object, which intensifies the procedure. It is further intensified when she says to him, *"I am happy to be a consultant to you. All other responsibilities I hereby return to you."* Afterwards, there is some clarification of the relationship between her and the new boss. (We remember the first configuration where the scene seemed more like the consultant was "bringing up" the new boss than in a business relationship with him.) To help define and emphasise the level of their relationship, we suggest the sentence, *"You're the new boss and I am your business consultant. I've got something confused. I'm sorry!"* The new boss says in turn, *"I am your client and I respect you as my business consultant. I've got something confused also. I'm sorry!"*

In the uttering of sentences of resolution, the coach takes care that the representative does not merely repeat the words, but also feels the sentences. We are not dealing with the exchange of information here (which is known anyway), but with dissolving an inappropriate and unconscious amalgamation of emotions. The coach can see by the reaction of the representatives whether this has been successful.

Both representatives nod to each other, much relieved. Now Ms M can retreat into a neutral position as an observer. Everyone in the circle exhales and relaxes, especially the new boss.

After this clearing work, he feels more serious. His rebellious attitude is gone. The representatives of the new and old boss stand facing each other for the next step. The successor says to the retiring boss, *"You continue to be important to all of us as the head of the organisation."* He indicates the other directors as he says this. In the next step he adds, *"You are the old boss and I am your future replacement. When I need the advice of an 'old hand' I'll come to you."*

The clarifying definition of relationships helps the old boss as well. *"You are my successor, but as long as I am still in the firm, I am still your boss. I will gladly help you prepare for your future role."*

After this process work, the representatives of Directors A and B no longer feel fixated on the consultant. Their mistrust of the new boss has melted. They look at their old boss with respect.

In the course of the process work, the representative of the bank's customers has calmed down some, but remains sceptical.

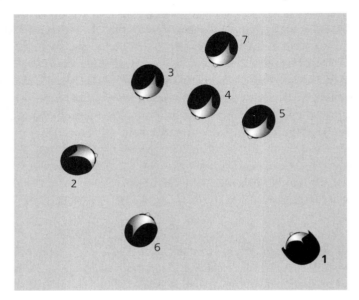

1	The business consultant, Ms M	5	Director B
2	The old boss	6	The bank's customers
3	The new boss	7	The entire firm
4	Director A		

Fig. 2: The picture of resolution

Ms M

The representative of Ms M is now able to assume a position from which she has an overview for her consulting function. She finds a place where she can see everyone, but where she remains outside the bank's system.

The old boss

The old boss can now step back into his leadership role and take a place in the picture of resolution that is appropriate to his position.

As chairman of the board he stands to the far right. It is important for him to keep some distance from his successor, the new boss.

The new boss

The new boss stands to the left of the old boss. In this position he feels serious and responsible. With eye contact with his consultant, who is standing some distance away, he says, *"I can imagine a working relationship like this."*

Directors A and B

Both representatives of directors A and B are standing to the left of the new boss. Their position is the same but their feelings have changed. Their mistrust and anger towards the new boss are gone. Both can easily see the old boss. They no longer feel any need for close contact with the consultant.

The bank's customers

The representative of the bank's customers now has a place in the system where everyone is aware of him.

When the resolution has been set up in this form, the representatives of the new boss and the other two directors complain that something is missing behind them. We add a representative for the *entire firm* (position 7) behind them and they feel supported.

This is a particularly succinct example of how the physical awareness of the representatives in their roles can point to systemic gaps.

Ms M herself

We now ask Ms M to take her representative's place in the picture of resolution.

Coach: Ms M, how is this new position?
Ms M: Unusual, in that it's so far out. But I have a better overview from here. (She looks sceptically at the representative of the new boss.)
Coach: Is there something you still need to clear up with him? (indicating the new boss)
Ms M: I don't know but I don't quite trust this peace with him.
Coach: Would you like to try something?

Ms M: Why not?

Coach: Stand facing him, look directly at him and say, "I have let myself be very hurt by you. I am still carrying something of a grudge. Please be understanding if I pull back a while as your consultant."

Ms M speaks these sentences in a very accusatory tone. The representative of the new boss immediately expresses his protest in body language.

Coach: Did you notice what happened?
Ms M: Yes, you couldn't miss his reaction!
Coach: Let's go one step further. Are you with us?

The consultant looks round the circle, nods and says, "Okay!"

Coach: Close your eyes for a moment. Pay attention to your body. Notice how you are standing and whether it's comfortable. If not, change your position. Make contact with the part of you that is clear, competent, objective, impersonal and therefore, successful. Can you find that part of you?

After a while, she nods.

Coach: Now think of a situation where you were exactly like that: clear, competent, objective, impersonal and therefore successful. Get a clear image of that situation in every detail!

As the consultant nods, the coach helps her to experience this situation completely, using all five senses. It is clear from her non-verbal feedback that she has been able to do this.

Coach: Fine. Open your eyes again and take some time to get your orientation in the room. Now look at the representative of the new boss again. Connect, as you have just done, to the part of your personality that is clear, competent, objective, and impersonal. Now say once more the following sentences, "I have let myself be very hurt by you. I am still carrying something of a grudge. Please be understanding if I pull back a while as your consultant."

Standing tall, she repeats these sentences in a friendly but neutral tone. It is clear from the body language of the new boss's representative that he is now able to take in what she is saying.

Ms M (adds a sentence of her own): I've got something confused there. I don't know what, but that is my issue and has nothing to do with our working relationship.

We ask the representative of the new boss to affirm, *"I too have got something confused here that has nothing to do with our working relationship. I'm sorry."*

Ms M appears visibly more relaxed. She has now cleared her mind and we recommend that she look round once more, noting particularly this outside position as consultant, and anchor that awareness in herself. When she has released the representatives from their roles, we end the constellation.

The dynamics

The old boss was in a weak position in relation to his successor and the other directors. With his attitude of "we're all equals on the board" he was no longer in touch with his position as head of the bank. A transfer of authority to his successor was impossible because he had already abdicated his authority. He could not pass on what he didn't have! The consultant unconsciously moved into the authority vacuum to compensate. She got in so far that she was pulled into the system and slid into an undercover leadership role. By unspoken but mutual agreement, her job description was altered – from consultant to hidden leader. The successor unconsciously rebelled against this secret boss and the lack of orientation of his predecessor, and expressed his rebellion behaviourally. Unconscious behaviour patterns also emerged between him and the consultant that exacerbated his rebellion and weakened her position in relation to him. He exhibited symptoms that made the problems in the system visible.

Violations of systemic principles

In this working system the order was disrupted when the old boss no longer carried the responsibility of his position and task, and put himself in a dependent, weak position in relation to his successor and to the other directors. Neither the priority of those who came first over those who came later, nor the higher ranking of the old boss's authority were attended to. The balance in the system could no longer function. The consultant was in a presumptuous leadership role, inappropriate to the reality of the situation. One could say that the relationships were truly "con-fused" and needed to be "de-fused". The fusion was dissolved and the rebellion was defused when the consultant returned to an appropriate position outside, which helped to relieve the system.

Implementation in practice

The consultant had a clearing discussion with her client in which she clearly defined her role as an external expert. They worked out and clarified new guidelines for her job.

The old boss and the new boss came to a clear working agreement. The current chairman of the board resumed his authority until such time as he left the firm. He also offered his services as the "old hand" for advice and assistance when needed.

Through systemic coaching, the incoming boss identified the part of his personality that had reacted with rebellion and defiance and thus gained a broader perspective for himself for the future.

Ms M also opted to have some coaching in order to identify what part of her had accepted this hidden role of authority and what had got entangled in her client's relationship patterns (see Chapter 5.2).

3.6 "WHERE AM I HEADING?"
A SUCCESSFUL PROFESSIONAL AT A FORK IN THE ROAD

Background information

Ms S had worked in a well-known international software company for eight years. As head of a team and a qualified specialist, she and her colleagues had produced valuable work in development for the company. Many of the innovative products for which the firm was renowned were due to the initiative and performance of her team.

In her position, she was particularly supportive of young colleagues because she recognised the importance of the innovative potential of these young software engineers for the future of the firm. For this reason, one of her innovations was a creative circle in which her young colleagues were freed up from customer projects so they could develop their own ideas and visions.

Conflicts with management

This practice did not meet with unequivocal support. Particularly problematic for her was the relationship with two managers who represented a more pragmatic, sales-orientated line. They had little understanding for her time-consuming and non-productive team projects. The battle lines were clearly drawn and were noticeable at various levels in their daily work together. For example, the minimum time that Ms S deemed necessary for her and her team to develop a good product was continually shortened by the business manager so that the products could be put on the market faster. Not surprisingly, being "quick off the mark" resulted in quality problems. Customer complaints and their anger in response to these shortcomings landed on the hot-line desk, which was supervised by Ms S. Her intercessions with the business manager brought about no change. In her opinion, the concessions to sales volume imposed such limitations on her and her team that she saw declining prospects for the future of the company. She was also hurt by the sarcastic, condescending tone used by one of the managers whenever he spoke to her.

Ms S began to think about a career move and discovered that her chances in the open market looked very promising. Besides her technical expertise, there was a high demand for people interested in teamwork and innovation – precisely her own priorities! Nonetheless, she was worried about making a change that might mean jumping from the frying pan to the fire.

As an alternative she was also considering going free-lance or starting her own business. The freedom and opportunity to make her own decisions was attractive, but the risks were considerable in a highly competitive market. She was spoilt for choice.

Because of a personal issue some years earlier, Ms S had taken part in a seminar for family constellations. As the seminar had helped her to gain clarity in a difficult situation, she decided to try to get some perspective on this professional dilemma through a systemic constellation.

Systemically orientated intervention
Ms S was not primarily interested in solving a problem; she was trying to get some clarity regarding her own future career and wanted a chance to look carefully at her options. When we had gathered the necessary information for the constellation, we decided on a particular constellation form that we call a "company culture constellation".*

---

* This form of constellation is attributed to Varga von Kibéd and Sparrer, who called it a constellation of polarities of beliefs.

In a company culture constellation, in addition to the people and organisations involved, higher values and principles are also represented.

We chose this form of constellation because in this case it is not only a question of a career difficulty, but a values choice as well.

Sparrer and M. Varga von Kibéd point to the importance of basic values as resources in organisations and note that certain problems in organisations are connected to a disregard for a basic value. Regardless of the concrete ideological orientation of a company, it appears that an organisation can only function harmoniously when three basic principles are respected.

Basic Values in Organisations

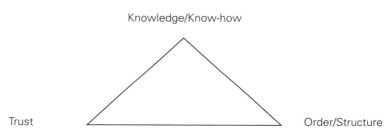

Knowledge/Know-how

Trust   Order/Structure

Giving priority to one of the basic values while neglecting others can cause destabilisation in an organisation.

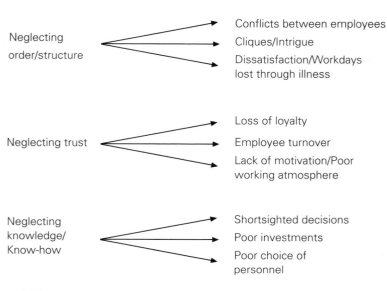

Neglecting order/structure

Conflicts between employees

Cliques/Intrigue

Dissatisfaction/Workdays lost through illness

Neglecting trust

Loss of loyalty

Employee turnover

Lack of motivation/Poor working atmosphere

Neglecting knowledge/Know-how

Shortsighted decisions

Poor investments

Poor choice of personnel

A balance between values

The qualities that are important to Ms S are trust, openness, empathy and team spirit. A constant focus on productivity, such as she sees in the two managers in her firm, is difficult for her to work with. She experiences these two bosses as narrow-minded, inflexible and strongly profit-orientated. At the same time however this attitude causes her to unconsciously reject the positive aspects of those principles, which are beneficial to the system. Because she so strongly identifies with her own value system, she can only see the negative side of the opposing pole of structure, order and security (see also Chapter 5.2).

In a balanced organisational culture, the opposing principles such as order, trust and knowledge complement one another. The same balance is just as critical in personal value systems.

From the philosophies of many different cultures and traditions we are presented with the triangle of truth, goodness and beauty, which can be read, more pragmatically, as knowledge, trust and order (know-how, team spirit and structure). An acceptance of the opposing poles is one requirement for equilibrium and stability within this field.

The German philosopher Friedrich Nietzsche presented this theme in the vivid analogy of the Greek gods Apollo and Dionysus. In ancient Greece, everyone was required to honour the gods. Individuals were allowed to turn to their favourites, but they had to also consider the gods who were not as appealing to them. A follower of the rational, disciplined Apollo also had to give sacrifices to the merry, wine-swilling Dionysus and his Bacchants, if he did not wish to suffer the vengeance of the insulted Dionysus. One had to at least dance a little Dionysus dance now and again in order to continue one's life as an Apollo fan undisturbed.

Likewise those who have a strong preference for structure and order have to learn to respect the principles of trust and know-how or innovation. On the other hand someone like Ms S who is flying the flag of trust and innovation needs the complementary principles of structure and order.

To give Ms S a chance to balance her personal value system, we add the three basic principles to the representations of persons and functions. We refer to these principles as *know-how, structure* and *trust.*

The constellation

Ms S formulates her issue for the constellation as, *"Where am I heading? Should I stay where I am despite the conflicts and limitations or should I find another job? Or should I take the big step and go independent?"* She then chooses representatives from the group of participants for the following:

- *She, herself,* referred to in the constellation as Ms S
- *The company she now works for*
- *Another company that she might work for,* referred to in the constellation as "new company"
- *Self-employment*
- *The trust principle,* empathy, openness, ability to work well with others
- *The knowledge principle,* clarity, insight, know-how – referred to in the constellation as know-how
- *The structure principle,* order, duty, negotiation, basic survival security

Ms S positions the representatives according to her inner image.

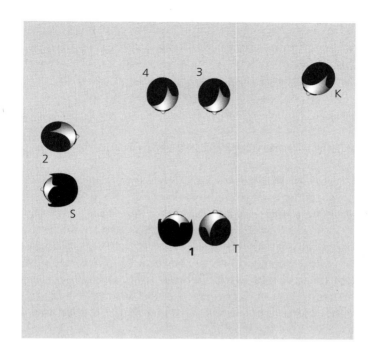

1 Ms S	K Know-how
2 Current company	T Trust
3 Possible new company	S Structure
4 Self-employment	

Fig. 1: The situation as it is

The new company and self-employment are standing facing Ms S and are looking at her. The know-how principle is placed at some distance to the side, looking at Ms S and trust. Ms S has placed the trust principle very near to the right side of her own representative, also facing the same direction as Ms S. The current company is standing next to the structure principle, who is turned away.

Ms S

Coach: How is the representative of Ms S feeling?
Ms S: I feel unsure of myself and conflicted. I don't know where I should look. To my right there is something very familiar. My left side feels dead. When I look in front of me I get fixated on these four eyes. I feel tension off to my left side, in the direction of the represen-

113

tative of my current company. I don't feel much of anything towards the knowledge principle. When I look this direction though, (indicates the structure principle, who is facing the other way) I am flooded with a combination of grief, anger and defiance.

Coach: "Trust" is standing very close to you. Is that pleasant or unpleasant?

Ms S: Familiar, as I said, but too close. It is almost as if I were stuck fast there, as if we were welded together!

The principle of trust

Coach: How is the trust principle doing?

Trust: I feel very powerful and important here. I am a major support for her (indicates Ms S's representative). Still and all, this is too close for me. I would like a bit more distance between us, but I'm afraid that she would then fall down. No one else is of interest to me except the representative who is turned away from us. My focus is clearly right here (points to Ms S). I experience her (indicates the representative of the structure principle) as threatening. I'm glad that I only have to look at her back!

The principle of structure

Coach: What is happening with the structure principle?

Structure: The longer I stand here in this position, the angrier I feel. Shoving me off to the side isn't going to solve anything. I'll tell you, without me, nothing happens here!

Coach: Do you feel any urge to move in any way?

Structure: Yes, I'd like to turn around.

Coach: Do it. (The representative turns around.) What has changed for you?

Structure: This is much better!

Coach: Who or what else do you notice?

Structure: Well, I feel a connection with the current company, almost like a sibling relationship.

The current company

Coach: How do you feel?

Current company: I'm standing here shoved off to one side! How am I supposed to feel? I keep looking at Ms S but she won't look at me. I feel a connection to the know-how principle and to the structure principle here next to me. I don't care for that symbiotic relationship over there at all (indicates Ms S and trust).

Coach: What do you mean, you "don't care for" it?

Current company: I feel like saying to her, "If that's the way it is, then I don't need to work with you."

The new company

Coach: What about this duo here? You're both looking at Ms S.

New company: This is not a good place for me. I need to be further back. When I look this direction (points to Ms S), I see only that unit of her and trust together. I feel about the same as the current company. Not interested! As far as my competitor here on my right (self-employment), that's not bad at all, but I could be a bit further away from him. I feel interested in know-how and structure but they're too far away.

Self-employment: I feel much the same as the new company. With that set up (points to Ms S and trust) I'm not interested either. I also need to be further back.

The principle of know-how

Coach: What is the representative of the know-how principle aware of?

Know-how: It's difficult to have a clear sense in this position. I could best describe it as being simply here, neither weak nor strong.

Coach: Do you feel anything towards the other representatives?

Know-how: Envy! I envy trust. That would be exactly the place for me! Perhaps not so close, but near Ms S in any case. What would she be without me?

We ask Ms S, who has observed the constellation from the outside, if she has anything to add, or any questions.

Ms S: I am very surprised by what is emerging here. I recognise the attitude of the representative of my current company. It is something like that in reality, but of course not as openly. That's one of the reasons I've been considering changing jobs. It is just now becoming really clear to me! This first picture is very informative for me. What I would like to know is how I can get free of this bias (indicates the representative of trust). Also, how does this help my career decision? I can't see it yet.

We ask Ms S to hold that question until the end of the constellation. In terms of the resolution, we too could only make a guess at this point. The basic dynamics of the conflict are clear however in this first configuration. We move on to the process work in the next step.

The work in process – interim pictures

During the process work, the representative of Ms S is able to honour the structure principle and its values for the first time. She frees herself a bit from the over-identification with the trust principle, a relationship that appears in the constellation as almost symbiotic. At the same time, the trust principle also moves physically away from her. In the next step she acknowledges the current company and the know-how principle. She is aware that trust and openness have no basis without structure and order. The know-how principle is recognised when she says to him, *"I have always relied on you, so I had simply forgotten what I have achieved with your help. I now acknowledge how important you are for my professional success!"*

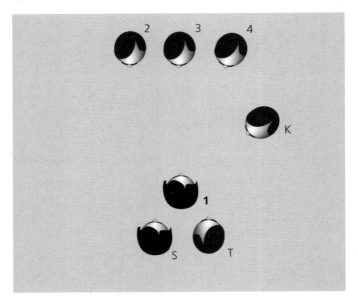

1	Ms S	4	Self-employment	S	Structure
2	Current company	K	Know-how		
3	Possible new company	T	Trust		

Fig. 2: The picture of resolution

116

The representative of Ms S seems relieved and freer. *"This support behind me gives me a lot of strength and the dead feeling on my left side is gone."*

The representatives of *trust* and *structure* stand behind the representative of Ms S as equally available resources for her. Saying, *"We're only available as a double-pack"* they give emphasis to their equal importance. The representative of the *know-how* principle feels best in a position where Ms S can easily see him.

The *current company, new company and self-employment* stand opposite Ms S at some distance from her. They are equidistant from her so that they carry equal weight. In this way she can take a serious, clear look at the three professional alternatives with their various pros and cons. Finally Ms S takes her representative's place in the constellation. She nods and says, *"That feels good. I feel the support behind me and having know-how on my right side is good."*

We ask her if she would like to try something more, and she agrees. We have her lean lightly against the representatives of structure and trust and physically feel the support. From this position, she then looks straight ahead at the three alternatives.

Ms S: (smiling in wonder) With this support behind me and with him (know-how) my perspective on things has suddenly changed. Those two (indicate the new company and self-employment) are not as attractive anymore. Yes, they're still there as possibilities, but just not as important. Also with him (indicates the current company) I don't feel so much resistance. I have one question though. What more can I do so that I don't fall back into that same trap as I go about my business? At the moment everything is quite clear!

Systemic coaching

In answer to her question, we suggest systemic coaching as an additional support to help her stabilise this new balance of values.

A fixation with one particular value may have a parallel in the person's family system. In coaching one can examine whether, for example, the individual feels a very strong loyalty to one parent or the other and to that parent's value system. If there is such a connection to one of the parents, the other parent, with his or her values, is often rejected. When those dynamics remain unconscious, it may become a life-long pattern and could prevent the individual from developing his or her own value system.

In a case where such dynamics dominate, it is difficult for an image of resolution to have the desired long-lasting effects.

Finally, we ask Ms S to release the representatives from their roles.

The dynamics

Ms S had an over-weighted bias towards trust, openness and inno-vation. Because she so strongly identified with these values, she was only able to see the principle of order as an obstacle and therefore felt compelled to reject it. More precisely, it was not the principle of order that she was rejecting, but the negative aspects such as nar-row-mindedness, rigidity and profit orientation. For her, the two managers represented these aspects, which moved her to fight against them. When she seemed to be losing the battle, she had no choice but to give up and pull back or to find a new job. The lopsided balance was aggravated by the fact that she did not reject the values of knowledge or know-how, but simply took them for granted. (She later explained that even as a child she was considered to be a "quick learner" and that had not changed as she grew up. That is perhaps why she had never paid much attention to this quality.)

She was able to establish a broader, more balanced value base when she could acknowledge the principle of structure and order as a fundamental support in her life, and become more consciously aware of her professional know-how as a valuable personal resource.

Violations of systemic principles

When the representatives of structure, survival, duty and order – in this case the managers in the current company – were rejected by Ms S, they reacted negatively towards her. She, in turn, was only able to see them as narrow-minded penny pinchers.

Those who work for the survival of the organisation have to be honoured in the system and given priority in the hierarchy.

Ms S found herself in an inappropriate position in the hierarchy, which primarily had a weakening effect on her.

Implementation of the solution in practice

We advise Ms S to approach her boss with her newly gained per-spective. She reports later that this manager, who had formerly been so cold towards her, now treats her in a very cooperative manner. She suspects that this has to do with her altered attitude towards the managers. Among other things, she now has some understanding for the priorities given to issues such as budget planning and rapid development, but still without being untrue to her own value sys-tem. The question of a job change has been set aside for the present.

4. The Value of Systemic Constellations – Questions and Answers from Seminars

Interesting and pertinent questions posed by participants in our open seminars or those attending lectures have helped us to focus our thoughts on systemic constellations. In this chapter we have put together some of the most frequently asked questions and our responses.

Turning the key

4.1 Turning the key to success – from problem to solution

Question: Can I resolve problems in a business with a single constellation?

Response: A constellation is not a magic pill. It is more like a key that you can use to open a door. However, it is not of much use if what I do is to open the door and then immediately look the other way and let the door slam shut again. I have to keep using my key again and again to open the door and look into the room behind it.

The image of resolution is like a glance through the opened door. You can see the situation without the problem and you see how things could be. At the same time, you know that you are not there yet, where you want to be. What you have got is a clear picture of your goal because you know what the solution looks like. With this image consciously in your mind, you go about your daily business.

In your everyday life you will recognise the familiar problems, but you can look at them differently. You no longer feel at the mercy of the miserable situation because you can see clearly where things are going astray. You get a clear picture of that from the first configuration in the constellation that shows the situation as it is. The final configuration, the picture of resolution, gives you an orientation for

119

the day-to-day work and strength to deal with it. It functions like a practical vision, spanning the gap between what is and what might be.

What do we mean by practical? For example, perhaps you now know that there has been a lot of competition and tension between development and production. Perhaps you suspected as much before the constellation, but the first as-is configuration and the feedback of the representatives have presented the situation very clearly right in front of your eyes. And you have probably seen an image of resolution in which development and production could work well together if they both kept their common goal in view.

You do not have to just wait until the solution appears in your company, because there are many things you can do to facilitate the process. In this case, a practical step would be to create interface teams between development and production, in which both sides can talk over the problems and their overriding common goals. The teams also learn concretely, in the sense of the resolution, to work together. A coach might be useful in supporting them to overcome their difficulties. Gradually both sides begin to find less constrained ways of working together towards their common goals. This development is contagious and soon their colleagues in both departments begin to feel the effects of the new wave. They too begin to dismantle their concept of each other as enemies. The energy that was previously expended in holding battle lines, can now be used in efforts towards a common goal.

Problems in information technology

Question: I work in the IT field, which is well known for being a fast moving industry. Can you use organisation constellations for systems that change rapidly?

Response: We can only set up a constellation of one business system with one situation, whether it is short lived or not. Even a randomly constructed system is subject to certain laws. For example, in a café you have a right to the place where you are sitting. If you leave that seat for ten minutes, you may very well have lost the right to sit there. In some organisational systems, the composition of members also changes very rapidly and that is not comparable to a structure that has developed over time. The fast and furious pace of the changes in IT leads to a feeling that "anything goes", with no long-

120

term thinking. The social connections are missing and people feel they are faced with a demand for complete and total flexibility. For the good of the company, they have to be prepared to give up social connections.

The magical word of the day, flexibility, puts a pretty face on one of the major difficulties of our time: the demand for a work force that can adapt in any direction, to any purpose in a global context. Munich today, next week a project in Singapore, followed by two months in New York, and so on. In a steady stream of coming and going and a constant change of important personal contacts, we can hardly build classical systemic structures. Such businesses are almost virtual, shapeless constructions, whose composition and visible form changes from day to day. In organisations that are structured this way, the power structure is efficient, but also formless – focus without centralisation.

To come back to the question, constellations of such systems are usually meaningful only in relation to the personal work situation of individuals. We have worked with a lot of IT people and in our experience, the presenting issue usually has to do with the individual, not with the company or team. There are questions such as, *"Is this company the right one for me?" "What is important to me in my professional life?"* The sense of belonging, with an attachment or loyalty to the company, is minimal. This raises the question for high-tech singles whizzing around the globe: *"Where do I experience any sense of belonging? Have I got social connections anywhere, or am I drifting completely unattached? Are people as arbitrarily exchangeable for me as chain hotels that look the same whether they are in America, Europe or Asia?"*

For personal issues of this nature, constellations are useful and meaningful. We have had good experience looking at issues of professional goals, and problem or dilemma situations using a certain type of constellation, which was developed by Matthias Varga von Kibéd and Insa Sparrer, called a systemic structure constellation. In these constellations, one can see quite clearly what is standing in the way of goals, what resources must be activated, and so on. When there is an issue of inner personal conflict, it is useful to set up a constellation of the micro-system, using representatives for the different parts of one personality.

Avoiding unnecessary conflict

Question: Is it possible to do the kind of constellations we have seen here in this open seminar directly in a company?

Response: Yes, it is possible. However, there are different conditions and requirements from those in an open seminar. Here we have a certain distance from the daily business of a company, you do not know most of the other participants and you share no common history. Even if you are here with a friend, there is a much greater willingness to express your own sensory awareness than there would be at your workplace, where there are various levels of relationship to be considered. Some things might feel embarrassing, or you might worry about unpleasant consequences if you were to speak as directly and honestly to your boss as what you have experienced here.

To avoid stirring up unnecessary conflicts, we use different procedures in a company than in an open seminar. For example we might use a constellation form that deals with themes rather than actual individuals.

If that is not possible, we allow different representatives, one after the other, to stand in the position of one person, which gives us a broader, more complete picture. It is immediately clear from the reactions of the representatives whether they are getting personal preferences or animosities mixed up in the role. The image is prettied up when someone sets up an artificially harmonious constellation in order to be polite, safe or considerate. When representatives follow a concept of their own rather than their sensory awareness, you get an empty image with no energy. These kinds of pictures, interestingly enough, have no meaningful impact. The representatives shrug their shoulders and have little awareness of anything. When that happens in an in-house constellation, we switch to another procedure or work in a one-to-one session.

What does your gut reaction tell you?

Question: You talk about goals coming back into view again in a constellation. Can this help me, practically, to clear away obstacles along the way to my goals?

Response: It often happens that everyone working on a project or team, or in a company, believes that the goals are clear and they are doing everything they can to reach them, but it simply isn't working; there is always one more hurdle standing in the way. That is the point when you ask the question about what would help achieve those goals. You would not ask that question if everything were going according to plan. If you want to get from Munich to Frankfurt, you get on the train or plane and get there. What I mean is, you do not usually give much thought to the possibility of the train going off the rails or the plane crashing, although these possibilities certainly exist. You just assume that you will get where you are going.

If you are thinking about this question, you are looking at the obstacles – perhaps something in the current market, in your company or in your own personality. The first step towards your goal would be to switch your attention from the obstacle course to the solution. We would then ask you exactly what you want to achieve and how you can know and test out concretely, if and when you have reached that goal. That is particularly important because even goals that are quantifiably measurable have a qualitative dimension.

It is the qualitative factor that makes the goals interesting to us. When a business manager says, for example, "We want to raise the sales volume by x% and lead the market!" he is naming a measurable quantity but he also has a subjective desire. The inner picture and feeling are what motivates, not the numbers!

How will you know if you are leading the market? The information does not just come from the Excel table that shows you the numbers compared to the competition. You feel it as well! Your "sixth sense", your "gut reaction" tell you if your company is really leading the market or if you are simply basking in a temporary, sunny spell of increased sales. Your surroundings also reflect the situation, with recognition or rejection.

When we use symbolic terms such as "gut reaction", we are unconsciously describing the systemic awareness that is common to everyone who belongs to the system of the business or organisation.

When we have concretely differentiated this "gut reaction" we could set up a constellation. We would begin with the appropriate setting; let's say for example, a constellation including you, your goal, the market, your customers and your employees. Let's assume that your representative in the constellation keeps looking at the competitors and ignores the goals. It would be very clear what movement is called for. Or perhaps we would set up your project team and look at how they stand in relation to one another. We might see how they prevent each other from moving towards the goal.

If we had the impression that your issue had to do with an inner conflict, we could set up the members of your inner team, aspects of your own personality. You might discover that a relatively weak part of you really wants to reach the goal, but a stronger part in the background is sabotaging the project. Once you know who on the inside and who on the outside sees the goal and wants to reach it and who does not, you have taken a large step forward.

Using the method as a complement to other consulting methods
Question: There are many different ways to iron out problems in a business. What distinguishes the systemic constellation from other approaches?
Response: The systemic constellation method works very well together in combination with other consulting approaches. The best time to use it is at the beginning of the consultation process, because it gives you valuable insights into the dynamics of an organisational system that might easily be overlooked otherwise. In a restructuring process, you could accidentally proceed down the wrong path if you did not know exactly how power in the firm is actually distributed.

In every business you find an official, formal power structure and an unofficial, informal one. The official version can be got from an organisational chart and fleshed out during interviews. As a consultant, you cannot get to the invisible dynamics *of the power structure in this way.*

This gives rise to the old consulting story that still amuses those in the field. *The consultants are to initiate cost-cutting measures in personnel, since many areas of the company are over-staffed. There are too many pigeons on the roof. So they clap their hands loudly and half of the pigeons fly away. The clients are delighted. The consultants have barely left the building when all the pigeons land on the roof again, right back in their old places.*

The pigeons know exactly where their place is! Systemic orders that have evolved over time will not allow themselves to be dislodged by some external push towards new innovation, no matter how much the consultant might want to believe it.

Regardless whether you are looking at personnel changes or a way to manage your supply chain more effectively, in our experience it is helpful to begin with a constellation. It gives you a clear picture in relation to the presenting issue. If you have already started something else to iron out rough spots in the company, for example managerial training procedures, we would include that as well. We start with the situation exactly as it is and let you look at it through a systemic constellation and consultation.

If an analysis has already been done or a change is already in process, our contribution is primarily to provide an analogue systemic picture. When you look at it, you know more than you did before. You can see clearly what the effects are – what is harmonising and strengthening the organisation and what is weakening, disrupting or producing tensions. You can then decide what is to happen next.

Harassment: Recognising systemic entanglements

Question: In our company, there are a lot of competitive struggles between individuals and departments. Could this method have an influence on that?

Response: When there is a lot of negative competition and exclusive cliques are having a destructive effect, this would be an indication of a systemic entanglement in the organisation. This is one of the classic applications of constellations, because they reveal very clearly what is going on. Usually a systemic principle has been violated, perhaps the balance of giving and taking; or perhaps there is someone with the right to belong, who has been excluded from the system, and now someone is being excluded in a different way, which brings the issue into the open.

In a case like that, a neutral setting is absolutely imperative. We could not possibly work with representatives who belong to the organisational system, because there is no way to know how involved they might be in the dynamics. If they were involved, they would not be representatives, but rather representatives of special interests. Issues involving harassment often have some personal family background, on the part of the victims as well as the perpetrators. When we suspect that this may be the case, we would opt for a family constellation in an appropriate setting. Of course this is only useful if the person or persons involved recognises the problem and wants to explore the issue to search for a solution.

Choosing a successor

Question: A department head is retiring from our company and we are facing the issue of whether to look in-house for a successor, or whether to find an external replacement. Would a constellation clarify that issue?

Response: To begin with, your question implies that this is not just a personnel decision. If you are not sure whether the successor to the position should be internal or external, it sounds as if the systemic conscience is at work. As you know, this conscience is a systemic sense of balance that automatically sounds an alarm when someone's right to belong is threatened. It could be that there is someone in your company who has a right to the position. If that were true, that right could not just be ignored without causing massive turbulence in the system. The facts of the situation would have to be checked out in a constellation before proceeding to the choice of a candidate. Now to the other part of your question:

A constellation of candidates can help in the process of making personnel choices. It complements and broadens the spectrum of methods used up to now, which often tend to be rational and linear. The systemic approach adds an important dimension, that of systemic awareness. In this way, space is made for interpersonal "chemistry", a quality that will play an important role in working together.

Personnel managers are often faced with the fact that, having hired someone with outstanding qualities, who came out on top in all assessment profiles, it turns out that the person just does not fit in the company. It is exactly this difficulty that can be illuminated beforehand with a constellation of candidates. In practice, representatives for various candidates are placed in the constellation in relation to their future boss, colleagues or employees. The members of the work system, the employees or higher management, often have surprisingly clear reactions. *"No, he doesn't fit here!"* Or, the representative elicits a smile and friendly welcome. The clarity and precision of the reactions to neutral representatives of candidates is astounding.

As we have said, traditional methods of choosing new personnel should also be continued, independently of the constellation. It is important that the head of the assessment centre not be involved in the constellation and also not be informed of the outcome until after the assessment has been concluded. In our work with personnel advisors, we have found that candidates who have been assessed positively and who were accepted in a test constellation, also fit into the company well in reality.

Question: We want to streamline our company and level out the present hierarchy. Would a constellation be useful in such a restructuring process?

Response: Well, a constellation will not streamline your company. It can depict the current situation, as it now stands, in relation to a specific issue. If you are asking if a particular approach to restructuring is useful, viewed systemically, you should check out first whether the rights of individuals or groups in the company might be violated. Whether we are talking about a level hierarchy or out-sourcing, the consequence is usually a reduction of the work force. When a company dismisses employees, the systemic question is always considered with an eye to the balance of giving and taking.

It makes a difference whether dismissals are unavoidable if the firm is to survive, or whether they serve only the interests of one group, such as shareholders. If the latter is true, it should be a warning signal, because a one-sided sacrifice by one group for the benefit of another group can throw the whole organisational system out of balance and provoke serious symptoms in the system.

The symptoms will correspond to the consequences suffered by those who have been ignored or pushed out of their place in the organisational system, but the symptoms may even be a bit more dramatic, as if to underscore the problem. It appears that a systemic conscience, as a compass for action, is not restricted to individual people, but also works for the whole.

Organisations' systems react with an uncanny precision, as if they want to compensate very exactly for a distorted balance – with compounded interest payments, so to speak. You might formulate the issue for a constellation as: *"I would like to steer our restructuring process in a way that does not disrupt the balance of giving and taking."* In doing this it also becomes clear who "we" are. Is it the managing director who says, *"We want to streamline,"* and on whose behalf is he speaking? Does he also mean his own waistline when he talks about the belt tightening to be done, or does he only mean the others? Who has he got behind him, and who is against him? A constellation can show all this very clearly and bring the issue into focus. These sorts of issues that affect all the members of the organisation have to be addressed with no beating around the bush, so everyone knows where they stand.

Causes of high employee turnover

Question: What is the systemic background for a high employee turnover in a company?

Response: That is not possible to answer. There could be various reasons, perhaps a weak connection to the company and very attractive rival companies, or it could have to do with a redistribution of the systemic balance. Without more detailed information we could only guess at the cause (see case example in Chapter 3 which concerns high employee turnover). Previous injuries to the system are often balanced by new damage. Of course that is of no use to anyone, but that is the way interpersonal systems function when the processes go on unconsciously, "underground". You can see how important it is to remain alert and aware of the systemic aspect, because it is the only way you will recognise negative movements and be in a position to take corrective measures.

If balance is not achieved through acknowledgement and respect, the organisation's system will destroy itself. Strangely enough, those involved will agree to the destruction and say, *"That's what has to happen!"* Their need for balance, which outweighs any consideration of success, is satisfied. Whether we like it or not, no one can put him or herself above the basic systemic principles. Nonetheless, the attempt occurs frequently, usually due to youthful over-confidence.

We have adopted a version of an ideal of management, drawn from an American "youth orientated" vision, of the dynamic 30-year-old "shooting star" who comes in as head of the business and transforms the company with a radiant, fresh energy. The consequences, however, are sometimes serious and expensive. Young managers, in fact, often have a good nose for quick profit, but seldom a good sense for rights and membership. What could happen is that a young manager may quickly gamble away what has taken generations to build up.

Of course experienced managers can also have destructive effects. When there are changes at the executive level it is particularly visible; you see extremely successful 50-somethings, who have invested everything in "their" company, only to leave the firm with huge financial settlements and switch to a rival company. Overnight, they convincingly defend the opposite of what they were fully committed to yesterday. That might be possible to understand systemically, if there was never a true sense of belonging to "their" company. They used the firm but, in reality, were only loyally bound to a different group – the group of international "top people".

128

4.2 Activating resources – individual and organisational growth

Seeing professional alternatives clearly

Question: I am facing an important professional decision and I don't know at the moment which way I'm going to go. There is much to be said for one option, but also for the other. In such a case is a constellation worthwhile to help to make the decision?

Response: Yes, decision-making is an area where systemic constellations are useful. They help to make the alternatives clearer and give you a new perspective with a bit of distance, so you can make your decision with more awareness. When we had fully understood what the issue is for you, we would ask what, in your opinion, would define a good result? Would A be just as possible for you as B? Perhaps there is a C or a D? In making decisions, it is a good idea not to limit your options too much at the beginning. Sometimes other possibilities become apparent once you look past your dilemma. We would suggest a particular kind of constellation that allows you to do just that. It is called a *Tetralemma*-constellation, and was developed by Varga von Kibéd and Sparrer.

In a dilemma, *you have two alternatives, one side and the other. In a tetralemma you expand your inner vision to include four positions: one side, the other sides, both sides and neither side. By removing yourself from the dilemma in this way, you can see more clearly what price each decision carries with it, and more easily find a creative solution.*

Conflicts in the inner team

Question: I have some personal goals that are very important to me, but I have the feeling that I'm standing in my own way and preventing myself from getting there. Is there a way to use this method to get a handle on that so that I can get to where I want to be?

Response: It is important to remember that we are connected to various interpersonal systems as well as our intrapersonal systems. The most important and most influential interpersonal system is the family, both our family of origin and the family that we establish as adults. Viewed systemically, family is the most important because we receive life from our family of origin, our parents; and we pass life on in our own family, to our children. In second place of importance is the work system, because it ensures our material survival.

Our intrapersonal system is powerful in the same way as the family, because it evolves very early in our lives, when we are growing up in our

129

family. Each of us has developed various aspects of personality to protect us and keep us safe. All together, these aspects comprise a single person.

Because our circumstances change in the course of our lives, from nursery school to professional life, what functioned well yesterday may not be useful tomorrow. Therefore, we have in ourselves parts of our personality that have power and parts that have lost power, and they struggle with one another just as the members of an inter-personal system. In one person there may be a part that is a self-confident, capable doer, and another side that is a sensitive musician. Or there is a continually nagging achiever in a struggle against a side who enjoys life to the utmost.

If you have the feeling that you are standing in your own way, it could be an expression of a conflict between two or more opposing parts of your own personality. It is very possible that your personal goals are important to only *one* part of your inner system, whereas other parts reject these goals.

We could check that out by setting up a constellation of some of the most important inner characteristics, as if they were separate people. From the picture of their relationship to one another and the feedback of the representatives, you get more information about what is going on. You can use individual coaching to deepen your understanding if needed.

The facts are enough.

Question: How far do I have to go into the details of a personal problem in my company; I mean, how intimately? Is it possible to work in this framework without exposing oneself to a striptease of the soul?

Response: In constellation work, your personal life is ensured protection. The details and personal characteristics of those involved are not necessary in order to get a clear picture; the facts suffice. We need to know actual facts such as: Who founded the company, with whom, or from whom was it purchased? When did individuals join the firm and what are their positions? Is there anyone who has been excluded or who might be? Has anyone sustained injury or been unjustly treated? Those are the kinds of things we need in order to work. In the systemic approach we are not analysing the problem, and more details would only distract the representatives from what is essential. We manage with very minimal personal information because we are focussed on the solution. For that we need a clear issue. We need to know which direction you are heading. Then we can work.

Family patterns are repeated.

Question: What role does your personal family background play in relation to professional or personal goals or problems? More importantly, how do you proceed when it appears from a constellation that your family background is involved?

Response: It happens more often than is generally thought that issues from someone's own family are repeated in a professional context. For example, if someone feels unjustly treated in their family, or has at some time rebelled in vain against their father, the individual goes into the office with that sense and often experiences a similar situation in the work environment. The boss is unconsciously seen as the father and evokes the same opposition, but of course he has no idea what is going on with his employee. Conflicts like this are inevitable.

Many interpersonal conflicts in the professional arena probably have their roots in an unconscious family background. In a constellation you can tell by the reaction of the representatives when it actually has to do with a family issue.

Sometimes, in a seminar for organisational constellations, it is also possible to go into family issues if the person doing the constellation agrees to it. It depends who the participants are and how much trust has developed in the group. When the setting is not appropriate, we talk to the person privately and suggest either individual coaching with us or a colleague, or a seminar for family constellations.

Good solutions aren't necessarily dramatic.

Question: I have had very good experience with family constellations, but in that setting things often become very emotional and dramatic before you get to resolution. Here on the other hand, it is very calm. Is the method effective anyway?

Response: The intense and dramatic feelings that you see in family constellations are often the feelings of a child. There, what comes up is the relationship of a small child to its mother or father and it is not unusual for that to be connected to a state of emergency in the soul, and it is normal for tears to flow. Or it may have to do with a difficult fate suffered by someone in the family – illness, early death or exclusion. When something like that appears in a constellation, it may result in powerful emotions. That is healing as you and many others have experienced.

In organisational constellations we are concerned with different issues. It is true that dramas also occur in businesses, and systemic principles are also violated; there is no question about it. But the emotional voltage is not as high. Membership in a firm is not due to the workings of fate. You can go to your boss and give notice and you're out. In a family that doesn't work – even when teenage rage causes doors to slam and provokes cries of "Don't come back!" Even if you move to another country and break off with your homeland, the inner bond to the family remains just as strong, perhaps even stronger than if you saw your parents and siblings on a daily basis.

The emotional depths and intensity reflect the system and the bonds that exist. That has nothing to do with finding good solutions. Resolution can also be found in a calm, relaxed atmosphere.

A clear vision of the future

Question: I want to develop a clear vision for the future and set up my company in a strategic way. How could a constellation help?
Response: Constellations are not only helpful for solving problems; they can also broaden horizons. There is a particular form of constellation work that is especially designed to look at those issues. We ask how you experience your company culture and about the values that are most important to you. We would work out with you, as concretely as possible, how you envision your strategically optimal business and how you would know if you were on the right path leading to vision. Then we would set up the most important factors, for example, your current company, your vision and certain aspects of the company culture. We use a time line, which goes from the past, through the present and into the future. If your vision is still somewhat vague at present, this can provide a clear picture.

Water the plants, not the weeds.

Question: What is the importance of a solution orientation in constellations?
Response: It is of critical importance. Constellations function only with a clearly defined issue. Either you are looking for a solution to a problem, you want to know how to clear away obstacles in your path, or you want to reach a new goal.

A solution orientation provides the direction for the work. Without a clear desire for resolution, there is no goal. Idle interest or curiosity is not enough for a constellation. They do not provide enough energy.

The representatives cannot feel their way into a role and they react with confusion, or the situation becomes simply silly.

If you have a problem but no desire for resolution, you can never get out of the sphere of the problem. It draws you back in like a magnet. You could spend years on a problem, looking at it from all sides, analysing it and gaining insight into it, but you will never solve it.

The more attention you give to a problem, the more you water the weeds. That is a problem orientation. With a solution orientation, you water the plants you want to grow. The weeds dry up on their own.

The process of learning takes time.

Question: Supposing I find an image of resolution for my issue here in this seminar, is that it? Or, is there something that continues on from there?

Response: That depends very much on the issue, the context in which it exists, and on the image of resolution. With purely personal issues, for example, a private decision, it may be that the image of resolution puts things in focus so clearly that you don't need to do anything more to deal with it. In that case, it's enough to perhaps call after a while to talk over the results. Be careful, though – an image of resolution is not a prescription for action. It shows you a path and gives you a new perspective in an intuitive, analogue way.

Images of resolution speak to your emotional intelligence, much in the way that a work of art does. Your logical, analytical mind wants a recipe for action and an instruction manual so that it can proceed, step by step, in the direction of the goal. Your intuitive intelligence takes in the picture and needs a period of incubation. Then after a while, the path and the goal are suddenly clear.

Our advice is to wait after a constellation and give the image of resolution a chance to work on you. It activates a learning field in you and in your surroundings, where your communication will now be somewhat changed. The term "learning organization" describes this process very well. First there is a stimulus, the input, which is the constellation, which then gives rise to a kind of learning process in the whole organisational field.

You need to give this process enough time and space, and you shouldn't expect that by next week your whole company will be

133

sorted out. The change in your viewpoint will have already created an effect, but you have to have patience. If you have questions later, it would be worth having an individual session in which we could track down the issues that are preventing the next step.

When dealing with complex business-related solutions, it is sometimes necessary to work out a plan with those involved, listing measures to be taken. This supports implementation of the solutions that have been found. One concept would include concrete steps to be taken within the firm – for example, open-space events, where everyone in the company comes together in small groups to talk over the up-coming changes, or forming teams at critical interfaces, or coaching for key personnel, or perhaps coordinating efforts with other projects and training to improve specific skills, such as communication or conflict mediation.

4.3 MORE THAN JUST BEING THERE – USING PARTICIPANTS' OBSERVATIONS

Holding systemic awareness in everyday life

Question: If someone does not have an issue, what value is there in being a representative or observer of a constellation?

Response: There can be of value at many levels. First of all, for those who are new to constellation work, participatory observation is a way to get acquainted with the work. In watching constellations done by others, you gradually become familiar with the procedure and begin to understand the systemic dynamics that appear. You may be chosen as a representative and get practice in feeling your way into the role. This is a way to sharpen your awareness and to learn to discriminate between your own opinions and the impulses and sensations of the representative role. That is a useful and important skill to acquire for your work as well. In discussions with employees or customers it is helpful if you are able to listen carefully, be aware of non-verbal reactions and to take off the filters of your own personal opinions and experience.

You also practice bridging feelings and rational thought, analytical thinking and intuitive understanding. You learn to feel your way into the role of a total stranger and in a depth that is rare in everyday life. Your social and emotional competence is trained in this way.

We have been told by participants who often work with us that they are quicker to understand their colleagues and customers and are more accepted and appreciated in their workplace. That is not really a surprise, since everyone reacts positively when they feel understood and accepted as they are. You broaden your leadership tools in another way as well; you learn to think and experience systemically.

The more instances and issues you observe in constellations, the more awake and alert you will be to violations of the basic principles and orders of work systems in your daily life. You will gradually develop an eye for systemic traps and learn to avoid them.

For instance if you are starting a new project involving various departments or branches, you pay attention to the systemic ranking. You recognise who can lead a team and who cannot. When one person is conspicuously problematic, you do not automatically attribute it to that person's personality, you check out whether the individual could be exhibiting symptoms on behalf of the whole system.

We have found in seminars that through participatory observation and acting as representative for others, you also gain perspective on your own questions and processes. Last week a participant came to us and jokingly expressed his disappointment: *"What a pity! I had prepared my issue so carefully, and then it all got taken care of without me. In the last constellation of Ms A, the same issue came up and now I'm absolutely clear about what is going on in my firm and what has to happen next."*

A further effect is what many participants have described as an *"expanded world view."* We have received letters with feedback such as: *"The experience with constellations has changed my perception of many problems. I no longer look for the guilty party but instead I notice the reciprocal effects in the system." "I found it fascinating to experience how an "intelligent field" connects people in a firm. My awareness of this effect has been heightened."*

Representatives are the temporary spokespersons for another system.

Question: How reliable is the feedback from representatives? Couldn't you arrive at a false conclusion if someone in a representative role is too impacted by his or her own background? If so, how do you handle that as a constellation leader?

Response: Naturally, representatives bring themselves into a role, but that relates more to the form of expression than it does the content.

Some people are more dramatic and lean towards a more theatrical expression. Others are quieter and express themselves with more reserve. It does not affect the essential content of what is being represented very much.

Most representatives, without any prior knowledge, are able to describe a situation more precisely than the person being represented – who is often amazed. That is because they have no personal reservations or interests invested in their feedback. They only reflect a systemic awareness that has proven to be helpful and useful.

A representative is a temporary spokesperson for an unfamiliar system. We have very rarely found that a representative has imported a completely different issue into a role. When it happens, it becomes evident very quickly because it does not fit into the relationship network in the system and the other representatives don't know what to do with it. In such a case we replace the representative and work with that representative's issue later.

There are other noticeable clues when a representative is not tuned in to the issue at hand. The person is not collected, which has an effect on the other representatives and the constellation cannot develop any energy. There again we replace the representative or interrupt the process; but it rarely happens.

A constellation leader needs a good eye and a lot of experience to be able to notice these things quickly and take charge before it gets out of hand.

The cure for sore muscles is more exercise.

Question: I find observing a constellation or acting as a representative very interesting and exciting, but at the same time, it is strenuous and tiring. Why is that?

Response: As a representative, you temporarily leave your own personal experience of the world and make yourself available for a particular role. You express feelings and sensations that could be diametrically opposed to your own normal experience. It is like inner stretching. You stretch yourself to encompass this new perspective. Stretching can cause sore muscles.

Or, perhaps you are sitting outside the circle, making an effort to follow all the different perspectives, positions and effects. You have to use the same inner tools – your skill in entering into another person's feelings. Experiencing the feelings of so many different people is good training for increased sensitivity and awareness but it's hard work, at least at the beginning. With time you also get more relaxed when you are observing or in a role. You identify less with the content, yours or someone else's, and you can take on a role with some inner distance. You can report the sensations without being unduly influenced by them, and you find a way to maintain a certain reserve. This is easier to do if you are well collected, which means that in the process of representing a role or observing, you are consciously directing your awareness both inwardly and outwardly at the same time. By the way, it is like what happens in sports; the only thing that helps sore muscles in to continue exercising!

Will you accept a bit less?

Question: I can see from the constellation what the solution would be, but is it that easy? Isn't there more involved?

Response: Imagine you are standing at the delicatessen counter and you order a very fine, very expensive cheese. You would like four pieces and the cheesemonger asks if you would accept a bit less. What's your reaction? You would probably be very taken aback! Why doesn't he want to sell more? There is certainly enough there! What seems absurd at the deli counter is reasonable in our context. *"Will you accept a bit less?"* is the question the solution-orientated consultant asks the client when the client wants more. Why? Attitudes we have learned in one context are easily carried over into other areas of life, without our checking out whether the behaviour is truly useful in the new situation. For example, in Germany after the war, when there was not enough food, the motto was, *"A lot helps a lot."* When starvation was no longer an issue, the over-eating of the 50's took over.

When it comes to solutions, a lot does not help a lot. More of the same is not more, but less – less effective! This is why the work in a constellation is so concise, almost minimalist. We do not set up the entire system, we begin with the factors that are directly involved. In the course of the constellation it becomes apparent if additional elements are needed. Even seemingly unsolvable problems sometimes have simple solutions.

It may be difficult to accept a simple solution, though. If we have suffered with a problem for a long time and invested a lot of energy trying to get rid of it, it has become a familiar companion by now and it is not so easy to leave it behind. Also, how would it be to have to admit that although a problem has plagued you for a long time, the way was cleared in a matter of minutes? That's a hard pill to swallow!

Actually, problems are useful; as long as they are present, we can't act and are not exposed to the dangers of success. For example, if my firm's profit balance doesn't allow for the risky expansion abroad that we have been planning, I don't have to worry about whether I'll be successful abroad.

This is an experience that is not restricted to business, as social workers well know. Their work with the homeless, drug addicts or convicts is an effort to help them out of their muddle, but it very seldom succeeds. An old prisoner once explained the situation to a group of psychologists. *"Look,"* he said, *"why should I go out and earn a living, get married, and all that? It never works out anyway! Here in the clink, nothing can happen to me."* As long as he stayed at the bottom, there was nowhere to fall, and he felt safe. Any rise in fortune was tied to the risk of a painful crash. Without money, without a job, without a wife, he was safe. *"If you've got nothing, you've got nothing to lose,"* sang Bob Dylan.

If you are freed of your problem, you have to show what you can do. If you are combating a difficult problem, everyone will nod sympathetically if you fail. "Of course. With that employee turnover and the state of the market, even the best manager couldn't achieve anything."

A famous quote from George Bernhard Shaw is, *"There are two tragedies in life. One is not to get your heart's desire. The other is to get it."* So, the question arises for each of us as to whether we need a big problem, or whether a bit less would do.

Invisible gains

Question: You were talking about the value of problems. In our firm there is a very high staff turnover and I can't in any way see how that is useful to us!

Response: The usefulness might be very deep and wide reaching. You may get some inkling if you ask, seriously and honestly, *"How would it be if a miracle happened and this stopped tomorrow, and all the employees remained happily in the company?"* What feelings come up with this fantasy? Do you feel overjoyed and relieved or do you feel worried and doubtful? If you feel rather uneasy, one might suspect that you – or the company – are profiting in some invisible way from a high staff turnover.

In this case, in addition to the involved parties in the constellation, we could add a representative of the "invisible gain". We could then look at how the other representatives react, how much influence this representation has and what role it plays in the system.

Breaking off is not the end.

Question: You broke off the constellation I did earlier. Aside from the fact that I feel a bit broken off myself in the matter, what should I do with this? How do I continue?

Response: We had to break off the constellation because important information about your firm was missing. Continuing would have been just groping in the dark, and wouldn't have given you anything. You are feeling disappointed, understandably. When a constellation is broken off, it is always uncomfortable and sometimes frustrating for the client. On the other hand, it does not really break off the process. Your question continues to work on you as it crystallises and sharpens. We have had the experience of participants calling a while after a broken-off constellation to tell us that they didn't need a constellation any more. The solution had suddenly become clear!

This is a further example of the intuitive, right-brain process of problem solving. There is a stimulus, in this case disappointment, and after the incubation phase a creative solution appears, practically out of the blue. There is of course no guarantee, but you don't always have a guarantee of solving a problem using logical, analytical methods either. It's a good thing we have two halves to our brain! If nothing useful comes from one side, the other jumps in.

Even when a solution has been found, it is always a good idea to double-check it with the other half of the brain. That is, check the solution that has been worked out logically with your intuition, and one that was arrived at intuitively with a careful analysis. Emotional and rational intelligence, together, form a whole that is more than the sum of its parts.

There is an Arabic saying: *"Trust in God, but always tether your camel!"*

4.4 THE LATEST MAGIC FORMULA? – CRITICAL QUESTIONS ABOUT THE CONSTELLATION METHODS

A patient waiting for the doctor cannot proceed.

Question: Is the systemic constellation method the new magic formula that will solve all our problems?

Response: No, it certainly is not. A "magic formula" implies that you get something from the outside that solves your problem for you, without you doing anything. That would be like lying on the operating table and asking us to *"Remove this superfluous appendix!"* This kind of attitude on the part of a patient leads no further. Even if the symptoms disappeared, it wouldn't mean that the problem had been solved, and any joy over the "solution" would be short-lived. In systemic work the task is to recognise what the symptoms are saying, and what fundamental disturbance they point towards. If we have a clear issue we can see that much in a constellation. Constellation leaders are not problem solvers in the sense of a doctor-patient relationship. As experts, they can guide you through a process of resolution but the responsibility still remains with you. After all, it is your internal or external system! You bring the issue and the willingness to seek a resolution. The coach puts know-how and experience at your disposal to guide you towards your goal, but as the client, you are responsible for the goal and the path. This is important because it is also a sign of respect for you as a client. A coach or trainer cannot take over for clients and presume to direct their lives. That would show a complete lack of understanding of the basic systemic principles. What does a constellation actually provide?

A constellation is an excellent instrument for summarising the situation at a glance. There is hardly another approach that can focus and clarify complex organisational issues or difficult personal concerns so quickly. In addition, the method also allows a picture of resolution to evolve. In the process of a constellation, we unravel entanglements and organise the system according to fundamental principles until it feels "in order". In this way, a constellation can provide concrete assistance to a team, a department, or a firm, for restoring order and getting back on track.

Not a method to promote manipulation

Question: That is all well and good, but, isn't it possible to manipulate an organisation using a systemic constellation?

Response: We have never seen it happen. Of course it would be theoretically possible to use this tool manipulatively; no method is safe from that. On the other hand, if someone wants to be manipulative, why go to the trouble of doing a constellation first, which could have the effect of alerting people to the manipulation? It would be easier to manipulate in day-to-day contact, since hardly anyone remains constantly on the alert. The threshold for manipulation is measurably lower in our everyday dealings with people than in a new procedure such as this where many people are initially sceptical and very much on the alert – poor conditions for manipulation!

If someone were deliberately presenting false information, the constellation simply would not function. The representatives would not get any images and wouldn't be able to feel their way into it.

It is difficult, if not impossible, to lie at this level. A lot is transmitted instinctively through body awareness, by an urge to move, or simply a feeling in the atmosphere. It would be very difficult to try to artificially create the intense atmosphere of a constellation.

Perhaps you have had the experience in a team meeting of trying to change the atmosphere in the room when everyone is sitting there depressed and frustrated.

If you wanted to speculate about manipulation, you could certainly think, *"We will use it for industrial espionage! We'll just set up a constellation of our rivals and we'll find out where their weak points are. Then we can out-manoeuvre them!"*

In practice, it is hard to imagine. In any case, up to now we have only seen workable constellations when a constructive, solution-orientated issue has arisen out of the system itself. Destructive ideas that come from outside the system are not solution-orientated. It would be a rather naïve approach anyway, comparable to trying to develop a "remote control" to use on other people. People often hope that techniques such as "reading" body language or using it intentionally to influence other or NLP techniques will be such a tool. It doesn't work. You cannot open people up the way you open oysters in order to devour them. The other person will unconsciously sense the hidden intent and pull back inside. We have inherited an instinct for danger from our evolutionary predecessors, the mammals. When the alarm goes off, we experience a rush of adrenaline and we do anything but open up, we flee, we fight or we play dead.

In addition, even successful manipulation rarely leads to satisfactory results. The main purpose is usually to be in a position equal to the competitors. For that you can set up a constellation of your own company and the competition and find a good position. You gain much that is useful to you in terms of your own strengths and weaknesses, but no "secrets" about the others.

Resolution also suffers from jet lag.

Question: What happens when you can't find a resolution? Has it all been a waste of time, then?

Response: Absolutely not! Finding a resolution is not like roulette, red or black, win or lose. The resolution is much more a part of a systemic process in which, for example, a business changes a structure that has ceased to be effective in order to fit in better with current conditions.

The process of resolution always has its own timing. Sometimes the apple is so ripe that a flick of the finger is sufficient to make it fall. Sometimes it needs a bit more time on the tree before harvest time.

Problems and crises can be useful. You can learn a lot that will be of future use from a high staff turnover or a drop in sales. It would be a pity to simply remove the symptoms without having understood what was involved. Likewise, in a constellation it may be very helpful if no solution emerges. The first configuration of the situation as it is becomes even more meaningful in that case. As light through a convex lens, it becomes highly focused. You go home with either a clear view of the problem, or of your desired outcome. The process then continues day-to-day and you accumulate more energy for the solution.

There is an old oriental parable about the motivation to find a solution. When you really want something, you are like a person dying of the heat, looking for a bucket of water. The more urgent it becomes, the more energy you put into finding a solution! If the constellation reveals no resolution, it may also mean that the issue was not pressing enough, was not clear and precise enough, or that important information was missing. In any event, the process continues on.

We have had the experience that participants who felt very frustrated in a seminar because they were unable to find a solution phone us after a while to say, *"I've got it! The solution was suddenly clear to me and so was how to get to it."* A process was, in a sense, continuing underground and one day the bubbling spring burst through the earth's surface. It's a bit like jet lag. You fly to America and get off the plane, but you're not really there yet. Your biorhythms are still at home and you need to suffer for a few days until they have sorted it out. Resolution sometimes has jet lag.

Different photos of the same house

Question: Has there been any research done with double or triple blind trials? For example, if I do a constellation here with a particular issue and then I take the same issue elsewhere and do it again with different representatives and a different leader, will I get the same results?

Response: Scientific research on systemic constellation work is still in the beginning stages; there are some interesting approaches but not yet enough hard data to be able to say: This is how it is! We have had experience with multiple blind trials, but not yet in a scientific format that would yield representative results.

Experiments in which constellations have been repeated with the same issue but different leaders and representatives have resulted in the same experiences.

This confirms that the fundamental dynamics of a system always emerge. The concrete configurations may look different, but what they express and where they lead are identical. It is as though you were to photograph a house from different angles, from the back the front, the side and from the air. You would get a different picture each time but they are all clearly photos of the same house.

Truth is a timid creature.

Question: I have heard it said that a constellation leader has to work without a goal or conscious intention. How does that fit together with a solution orientation?

Response: No, you do not work "without a goal". Constellation leaders have a very clear aim and that is to help find the best possible structure and communication for the interpersonal system set up in the constellation. In order to do that, however – and it sounds like a paradox – they must have no intention. Such an illogical procedure often meets with scepticism in our western culture, since we tend to equate "illogical" with "ineffective". That is erroneous thinking.

In ancient China, thousands of years ago, another very effective principle emerged: Do by not doing. It has nothing to do with laziness; it means to remain fully alert as you make space for the unknown. When we look for a solution, we are moving into unknown territory where there are no maps. Logical-linear thinking is valuable if we know the map coordinates of the resolution. In constellation work they are not available, no matter how many strikingly similar cases we have already seen. Pulling out solutions from earlier instances would be comparable to trying to find your way around Munich with a map of Hamburg.

Goal orientation in a constellation is similar to the technique of a good marksman, who aims at the target and waits to see what happens to the shot. If he shifts into wanting *to land a perfect shot, he tenses up and his hand jerks.*

Creative solutions are a surprise because they are not the result of a logical thought process; they suddenly appear after the period of incubation needed for the analogue, pictorial work of the right brain. If you look at someone during this phase you will see no action, and logical thinkers would perhaps maintain that nothing is happening. Einstein lay in the bath and blew bubbles through a clay pipe. What is that supposed to mean? Suddenly, in non-doing, with no intention, the solution appeared! Many great discoveries and many more small, practical solutions have dropped into human history in this way.

Einstein had learned to release his concept of a goal in the manner of a Japanese Zen archer. Constellation leaders also have to learn this skill. They have to be able to guide the development of a constellation calmly, without intention, and with fully collected energy. Sometimes it seems as if it were going to come to nothing. At those times, when the process appears to stagnate, it is quite a challenge to stay calm and collected and wait, instead of just doing something – anything. When you feel about ready to give up, the dynamics suddenly become visible.

You have to be prepared to go to the limit, and to face up to potential failure in a constellation. You have to accept success and failure equally. This is not something you can learn, but it does grow with more experience. If we intended to reach a particular goal, or thought, like a chess player, that we already knew from experience what the right move was, we would be presuming to be cleverer than the systemic whole that we actually serve. That would miss the essential core.

What exactly is an attitude of non-intention? Certainly it does not mean, *"I don't care!"* It means that we follow the development of the constellation process without preconceived opinions. Our attitude is similar to that of an empirical researcher, whose view of a foreign culture is *"it doesn't make any difference to me,"* in the very best sense of the phrase. It doesn't mean indifference; it means that I regard whatever dynamics appear as equally valid. Trainers who lead constellations are faced with a very demanding task. They have to know themselves well and have to have developed enough awareness, internal as well as external, so they do not react automatically – pro or con. It sounds simple – as a constellation itself looks effortless – but actually requires years of training, self-exploration and supervision.

If we were to ally ourselves with one particular person or viewpoint, we would never be able to recognise the dynamics of the system. We would look at everything through a pre-set filter and would be easily led to support a single interest, or we might find ourselves blinded by a particularly dramatic issue.

Systemic dynamics work invisibly and, even with the best of intentions, cannot be dragged into view. The truth is a timid creature and you have to treat it with respect and care or you will drive it away.

This careful handling of clients' issues is also called "phenomenological" because you are not following a concept or plan. You move along with whatever the constellation brings from moment to moment. If the dynamics are not clear, the constellation leader can test out several variations. The desire for resolution comes from the client who has presented the issue, and we have to consider it carefully. This is why we ask, for example, *"What exactly would be different if your desired solution appeared?"* Or, we might ask, *"How could you tell, concretely, if your problem were gone tomorrow?"*

In a business constellation recently, an executive had misused his power of attorney. His boss was outraged and was tempted to get rid of him. It turned out, however, that the man had not really acted egotistically, but for the good of the firm – albeit in a risky way. His intent was to avoid damage to the company. If we had internally joined forces with the apparently justifiable outrage, the man's method of dealing with things would not have been clear – to the detriment of the entire company system!

No secret knowledge

Question: Following a constellation, how should a person act at work? This is not clear to me. I now know what the solution to a certain problem could look like, but my colleagues don't know this. Couldn't that cause new problems?

Response: The most important thing is not to press down on the accelerator! Let's say that your project team have not been working well together lately. You would like to find a solution to the team problem for you and your co-workers. When you return to work after the constellation, your colleagues are naturally eager to hear what came up. At this point they are in a sensitive, weaker position because they don't yet know what awaits them. Some may be worried, thinking, *"Are there going to be big changes? Will they affect my job? Are we going to turn the whole place upside-down?"*

Don't make a big mystery of the results! It works best if you give a factual account and concentrate on the solution. For example, you could describe the effect that the image of resolution had on you. You can make it clear that what is involved here is a learning process for everyone in the company and that no one will be excluded. Or, you could explain some of the fundamental principles of systems such as belonging, or the higher ranking of those who came earlier over those who came later.

Most people understand these things right away, completely intuitively. If there are questions and criticism, it will help if you interpret them all as signs of interest, rather than to dismiss or ridicule the concerns. For those who are particularly interested, perhaps you could make it possible for them to take part in a seminar or arrange an in-house constellation. Gradually, the constellation will lose its mystery and will be seen in the company as what it is, a valuable tool.

This refers to a business-related constellation issue. When it comes to personal issues, concentrate on your own inner process. If you make this a topic of conversation, you will pull the plug on your own source of power and the process will run down. If possible, do not say anything about it; if you must say something, keep it brief and factual. Describe the external process, but not your personal process.

A good balance is better than trickery in the long run.

Question: You have mentioned that it is good for a company when systemic balance is attended to. When I look around me in the world, I get the impression that it isn't fairness that comes out on top, but ruthless rip-offs! Isn't a balance of giving and taking sort of a pipe-dream?

Response: You can't just look at it short-term. Balance is a higher principle, but it requires time. The laws of nature demonstrate that for us. The pendulum always swings the other way; it won't stay on one side just because that happens to be our favourite side. You can see it everywhere, in human lives as well as in nature. Our ecological problems are direct proof. Where there is overexploitation of natural resources, too much taking, we pay a high price for restoring balance.

The human mind has great difficulty accepting this simple, universal principle of balance. It thinks itself very clever and plays tricks. "Buy now – pay later!" Pull off a coup now and you're a winner forever. That is nothing but an illusion! We believe we can just take and enjoy, and leave the bill for someone else – the losers –, but the best we can manage is a postponement.

In the end there is a higher price to be paid back, including compounded interest. In the course of the globalisation process we have been starkly reminded of this. There is no place in the world to ban the rubbish of civilisation to, where it does not have an effect on us. A wealthy country such as the US grants itself the right to consume one quarter of the world's resources, and buys itself out of any reduction in emissions. What good is that going to do the Americans when their own quality of living drops because of the ozone hole and climatic catastrophes?

The clever rip-off artists you were speaking of live in a childlike happy-ending fantasy. In the Hollywood soap operas there are these rosy happy-endings where the lucky winners beam happily forever, and no one asks about what it costs. In reality, just at the last frame where the smiles of the rich, happy couple are frozen, life begins to recreate a balance with crashes, disasters and downpours.

Everything has its price, and none of us can avoid paying it. After you have watched system constellations for a while, you feel more willing to pay the price immediately, before the penalty payments are tacked on. Even the most cleverly hidden accounts and the most well camouflaged bribes will eventually show up. It might run smoothly for a long time, but then things get really expensive for the "clever" ones.

We recently consulted for a company in which the chairman of the board made himself a good profit on the sale of a company holding, at the expense of the other members of the board. He had handled the sale and had fiddled the contracts so smoothly that he came out gold plated, whereas his partners had only a big minus to show for it. Now, you could say, hats off to him! Cleverly done! Or, how stupid of the others to let him pull one over on them like that!

However, there are now massive problems showing up in the sold-off company, and the new owners are attempting to make the ex-board liable for compensation. If they succeed, he will end up with even less than the partners he cheated.

That may sound a bit moralistic, as in, "honesty pays in the long run," or the biblical, "An eye for an eye and a tooth for a tooth," but that is not what this is about. Basically, we cannot ignore the fact that human systems function according to a principle of balance. If you choose not to believe it, you will end up hurting only yourself. If you acknowledge it, you will be more successful in the long run.

4.5 QUESTIONS FROM PARTICIPANTS IN A BUSINESS SYMPOSIUM

The following questions were posed following a demonstration of an organisation constellation.

Implementation in practice

Question: When everyone in the constellation feels right, isn't it possible that the feeling is simply being "nice"? Can there be a conflict between the feeling of "rightness" and the feeling that it doesn't bring us any closer to our goal? Are there conflicts like this?

Response: Yes, there are. People who have learned to think technically and to work out solutions are particularly sceptical at first. Scepticism means that you look carefully and critically. That is the translation of the word. You are not asked to believe that this works. Looking exactly means taking in the image of this configuration of resolution that has evolved and that you have followed through its evolution. That takes you one step beyond scepticism. Further, you could ask for example, *"What could that mean, that production and sales are standing next to each other in the image of resolution?"* A possible practical step might be a joint team at the interface of their work. That would be one consequence of the constellation. Through the image of resolution, you get to concrete measures that can be implemented and controlled. When the image is translated into practical action, scepticism can be overcome.

I'll give you one more case example that shows the value of the image of resolution. In one firm we worked directly with the people involved in dealing with a question of succession. The designated replacement for the original boss came into the firm, and two groups had to work parallel for a period of time. Dissatisfaction and tension arose amongst the employees and they had questions such as: *"Which one is in control, the old one or the new one? What's going to happen to us? Are they going to sell out?"* It paralysed the work and many employees gave notice.

The constellation clearly revealed a very uneasy relationship between the two bosses. In response to our question, the client doing the constellation reported that the prickly relationship was not taken very seriously and had been pretty much disregarded. It was visibly clear that the relationship between the old and new bosses had to be sorted out in order for the whole situation to ease. That was taken care of and there was immediate improvement in the everyday working atmosphere.

We are working here with a method that is out of the ordinary. However, when you have overcome your initial hesitation or scepticism, you have a tool at your disposal that is very practical, effective and comprehensive for giving you a picture of the situation as it is, and in leading you towards a solution. We know of no other method that deals with the interpersonal level that can do this as quickly. That is one of the real advantages!

Process and resolution are important.

Question: We have just seen in this demo constellation that there is an initial position, then different positions in the middle, and then an end position. What is the importance of these three phases? In the difference between the beginning and the end, I could theoretically interpolate a process that I could initiate. Or, do I just look at the final position?

Response: In the in-between stages, we see steps in the process that are useful in the practical application. When we do an in-house constellation, we document the individual steps of the process and then consult with our clients about which of these steps has meaning in practical terms. The image of resolution in the constellation just now demonstrated how important it is for the consultant to remain outside the system and maintain a good overview of the whole thing. That is why we define the task very precisely together with our clients, and later discuss which steps are necessary to implement the solution that emerges. Sometimes there is nothing more to be done. In other cases, training measures are needed or systemic coaching. To answer your question:

149

All three phases are important: The situation as it is, the process leading towards resolution and the solution itself.

The initial formulation must be clear.

Question: Would you say that the initial situation, or the initial picture is not coincidental, but rather, a reflection of the relationship conflict that is very close to the reality of the situation?

Response: Yes, but we often check out the initial picture by having various people in the company set up the constellation independently from one another. Sometimes the pictures are different, but they all have a similar basis or dynamics, which is also confirmed by the statements of the representatives. In any case, to do the constellation, it is very important to have a concrete issue in relation to a solution. Otherwise the constellation won't work. The representatives will not be focused, or they will feel confused. Therefore, we take some time to work with the client doing the constellation to define and formulate the issue. If we achieve this, we can assume that the initial image in the constellation will present the inner picture of the conflict – or whatever the issue is – in an external form.

Help with personnel decisions

Question: Using this method, can you find out if someone is in the wrong place in the company? For example, say there is someone who works in the financial end of things and is wondering whether he or she wouldn't be more effective somewhere else.

Response: This method can be used supportively in such a case, and at two levels. First of all you can look at the external system involved. In your example, that would be the financial area and perhaps also other areas of responsibility. At the same time, in individual coaching we would look at the person's inner system. Are there particular talents, strengths and abilities that have not been called upon up to now? Are there resources that are not being used? These two processes run parallel until it becomes clear where the person feels drawn and where he or she is particularly valued by colleagues. The issue is approached at different levels until a solution is found that considers both the organisational system and the personality structure of the individual. That may sound complicated, but in practice it can be accomplished with one constellation and a few coaching sessions.

150

In situations involving hiring new personnel, we use constellations to work cooperatively with those in charge of personnel decisions. One possible application is for determining which candidate would fit best into the existing team. In a constellation, representatives take the roles of the various candidates being considered and we can see how the existing team reacts to the various candidates.

For example, in a constellation perhaps the first candidate attracts everyone's interest, but the second candidate produces no reaction of interest, and the third is even rejected. Of course, independent of the constellation, you have to check this out using other procedures as well, carried out by neutral persons, perhaps using the tools of an assessment centre.

Breaking old habits

Question: What if an image of resolution is found but after a period of time everything slides back into the old structures. Does that happen?

Response: Yes, it can happen that old structures take over again. You can think of the picture of resolution as a key. One turn of the key does not always open the door wide and hold it open. The image of resolution tells you only that if you use the key the door will open. We humans are creatures of habit, and habits are notoriously durable. Often, we let the door to the solution close. Then it is useful to have a key to use to open it again. You keep opening the door until everyone involved sees where it leads. But you cannot expect that a one-off constellation will immediately sort everything out. That sometimes happens, but usually it takes a bit more work. In any case, you gain a clear view of the situation as it is, and that is worth a lot!

Changing goals

Question: If the goals have changed after one or two years, should you do another constellation?

Response: If there is a concrete issue that needs attention, yes, then we could look at the new goals. You can see at a glance in the constellation what changes these goals produce. Who finds this attractive, and who doesn't? What is needed to achieve these new goals? If something serious shows up, you can make corrections in time. You can make goal-orientated, precise decisions about which direction you want to move and where you want to invest; it can help you to determine preferences or the status of a new project.

5. Systemic Coaching – From Macro- to Micro-systems

5.1 HOW MACRO-SYSTEMS AND MICRO-SYSTEMS FIT TOGETHER

Concrete measures help to implement solutions.

In the previous chapters you have seen how system dynamics work in organisations and business and how they can be brought into order using the constellation method. As powerful and motivating as the images of resolution are in a constellation, they are not solutions that are already in place, nor are they instructions for proceeding. They provide compact information about a system and its development.

Is the image of resolution all that is needed? Are we to then just trust to its effects and go about our business as usual? Sometimes the resolution in a system constellation makes such a positive impression that it leaves little question about its implementation later. In other cases, concrete measures are needed to put a solution into practice. Those might include expanding a range of responsibilities, promotions, salary adjustments, or the creation of interface teams between conflicting parties in the firm.

Success also depends on the micro-system of the personality.

We are often asked by our clients, *"But what about the people who are essential for the implementation of the solution. They aren't going to just change!"* This is certainly true. That is why it is a good idea to extend the consulting task to include systemic coaching. It's possible for anyone to unintentionally sabotage a desired solution, even operating with all good intentions.

This is the meeting of two worlds that have a very special relationship to one another. The macro-system is the business with its multi-layered organisational structure. The micro-system is the personality with an equally complex "inner team" structure and numerous, often contradictory sub-personalities.

The question is which member of the "inner team" is the part of the person that has agreed to the solution and which part rejects it. In situations where it is called for, we look for the answer to this question in individual coaching sessions.

In the following section we will describe our approach to systemic coaching, which we have developed as a bridge between the collective and the individual worlds. The fundamentals are simple and proven. It is based on one of the oldest insights in human culture, the core of the *Emerald Tablet* of Hermes Trismegistos: *"As above, so below"*. Macrocosm and microcosm correspond. The structures and constellations that the ancients found in the cycles of nature, the orbiting of the planets, and in inner contemplation reflected a common fundamental order. Just as a single bird moves as a part of a huge flock, the organs and cells of the bird's body are subject to the laws of the larger system they belong to.

The whole is reflected in each of the parts.

One name for these basic building blocks of nature is "holons". They are organized according to the principle of "holons in holons in holons" (Ken Wilber). Every embryo passes through the entire evolution of life at fast speed, and after the birth is the child of its parents, of its culture and of its time. "As above, so below", means that as it is in the larger context, so it is in the smaller; as it is in the whole, so it is in the parts; *"the one is reflected in all"*.

This ancient philosophical theme is confirmed in many ways in the present. Scientists have discovered corresponding phenomena of macro- and micro-systems in molecular biology, biochemistry, genetic research and quantum physics. The smallest systems are recognisable as miniature editions of the whole. Our social and technological development also reflects this basic systemic principle.

A current example of such a macro-micro-reciprocity is the development of the Internet. In the network of x million computers lies the emergence of a macro-system, and we are just now beginning to have some idea of what the effects this has on the micro-system of our daily life and work.

Systemic micro-coaching helps remove obstacles.

In systemic coaching, we can use the corresponding macro- and micro-systems to support the implementation process of a systemic solution. As is true of any interface, the interaction between the organisational system and the individual system maybe a problem area. How can you implement an effective solution in the classic conflicting fields of individual interests and the goals of the team? The blind spots of an organisation, the unconscious obstacles in a company, can be revealed using the constellation method. You can see clearly how unproductive power struggles arise out of systemic entanglements and how you can improve the effectiveness of teamwork through a better positioning of the team members.

But how can you track your own inner power struggles? How can you ensure that the parties involved will accept the systemically optimal positions that have been discovered? Each individual is connected to the organisation's system, but also strongly influenced by other systemic forces, primarily their own family system and the inner system of their own personality. Coaching is an important tool for dealing with the fields of conflict that arise, offering individual guidance in systemic processes.

Macro- (families, businesses, organisations) and micro-systems (personality, with its "inner team" structure) are parallel systems that function according to similar fundamental patterns. The approaches to resolution that we have presented have been in response to either the macro-system of the company, or the micro-system of the person. Now matter how good the results may be, they are not comprehensive enough, because each neglects the other half.

Solutions must take both macro- and *micro-systems into consideration.*

In macro-micro-coaching, we integrate the work with both systems into a comprehensive, solution-orientated process. We begin with the systemic "as is" analysis at whatever point "the shoe pinches". If it is in the macro-system of the business, we look there for a solution. It becomes clear later in the departments, work groups and small teams whether that solution will hold. If there is a need for further intervention, we focus the coaching on the question: *"Do the individuals experience the macro-solution as a gain in their personal work situation? If not, what is needed to make a macro-solution acceptable to all?* The individual steps that were made in the constellation process provide clear indications towards solutions within the system of the personality.

5.2 HIDDEN POTENTIAL — THE HARMONY OF OPPOSITES

Difficult people are our best "trainers".

It is said that opposites attract. But they sometimes also collide violently and stir up conflicts. That primarily happens when one of the most important of the basic systemic principles has been ignored – recognising and acknowledging the other. Unfortunately, that is often exactly what happens. It is quite easy for us to acknowledge others who share our "pole", but considerably more difficult when it has to do with the opposite pole. That requires some practice, and do you know who your best trainer for that is? The person you cannot stand! Whatever it is in this person that is particularly abhorrent to you is the shadow side of what you are missing in yourself. An extra bonus from such a "trainer" is that you do not have to pay him or her! We would like to show you how you can use the characteristics in your image of the "enemy" for your own development. This is a particularly important process for dealing with work systems. If you can transform a condescending or disapproving attitude between production and sales into mutual respect, it clears a huge rock from the path.

The learning organisation is reflected in the atmosphere of the communication.

The picture of the situation as it is, in a constellation, shows you exactly where and how systemic entanglements or a neglect of systemic principles may be standing in the way of your success. In the image of resolution, you can see yourself at your goal, but in order to concretely implement the vision that is revealed there, it may be necessary to move from the macro- to the micro-system. When you can anchor the process of resolution in the organisation, concretely and practically, then the organisation begins to learn.

The learning organisation *can be seen in the micro-systems in the thinking, attitudes and actions of the employees.*

In the following section, a case example will introduce the "development square", which provides the first step into the micro-system.

Hubert Scrimp and his spendthrift business partner

Looking at another's "mistakes" covers up your own.

Hubert Scrimp and his business partner, Sam Splurge, managed a successful company, but Mr Scrimp disapproved of his partner's "addiction" to spending. He found it painful when Mr Splurge always had to have the very latest in office equipment and furnishings, whereas he made do with the same durable, solid furnishings he had had since the firm was founded fifteen years earlier. Mr Scrimp saw himself as a frugal, cool pragmatist. Although his partner was otherwise much appreciated, his spendthrift ways were a continual thorn in Mr Scrimp's side. When he looked at Mr Splurge's behaviour, Mr Scrimp could only see the opposite of his own frugality and only the negative side – this compulsive spending. The positive side of this quality, namely generosity, was not visible to him nor was the dark side of himself, his stinginess.

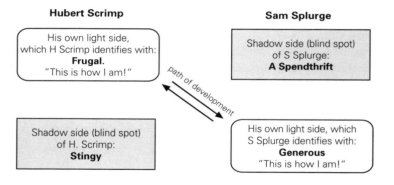

The shadow side distorts a vision of reality.

In this example, Mr Scrimp is dominated by the part of his personality that is identified with frugality. Because he is unaware of this identification, that part of his "inner team" takes over the controls and speaks out in his name against "spendthrifts". Mr Splurge, who Mr Scrimp has labelled as a spendthrift, sees himself as generous. For him, the dark side of generosity remains a blind spot. Sam Splurge sometimes worries about the chronic deficit in his personal budget, but under no circumstances would he want to be miserly like Hubert Scrimp!

Mr Splurge's light side is his generosity, a quality that has served him well in defusing conflict situations and in attracting new customers. The thrifty, practical Mr Scrimp is completely lacking in this quality. When Sam Splurge looks at Hubert Scrimp's frugality, all he can see is the shadow side, the stinginess.

As long as Mr Scrimp disapproves of his partner's "compulsion to spend", the light side of this quality, the generosity, is unavailable to him and he is constantly discomfited by Sam Splurge's carefree attitude. An ability to handle money in an appropriately generous way is seen only through the polarity of wasteful spending.

The inner solution has external effects.

If Mr Scrimp can dissolve his firm identification with frugality, he will be able to understand Mr Splurge's point of view without over-weighting the negative aspects. Then his black and white picture will change to allow him to see the positive side as well. He is then in a position that would allow him to loosen up his tight grip on his own budgeting and perhaps spend some of his money on the occasional luxury.

Mr Splurge then ceases to be seen exclusively as a compulsive spender. As Hubert Scrimp begins to let a quality of generosity into his own self-image and tentatively starts to experiment with this side, he also begins to be aware of a broader picture of Mr Splurge, without seeing only the exaggerated quality of a "spendthrift". This results in Mr Splurge finding new interest in Mr Scrimp's budgeting system because he feels Mr Scrimp's increasing good will and decreasing criticism. He also feels appreciated. Mutual understanding develops, which is advantageous for the firm as well.

This process is not only useful for improving communication between individuals, but also groups, businesses and institutions; it is a process that could help even countries and whole cultures to support the task of mutual understanding.

An intercultural win-win situation

We would like to return to the case of the company merger presented in Chapter 3.3. In the systemic constellation and follow-up sessions it was clear how important it is in a merger to respect the sensibilities of the smaller partner. Particularly when there are cultural differences, both sides tend to notice only the shadow side of the other and not the positive aspects.

The company uses the results of the constellation as an impetus to move intensively into intercultural relationship management. In

German-French communications training, both sides learn to broaden their views of the other culture. The model of the development square presented above helps to detect and redress over-weighting of particular qualities. In the joint IT project, the French initially saw the Germans as rigid technocrats who stubbornly insisted on their rules.

In this shadow side, the French not only rejected the perceived negative "German" qualities, but also blocked their own access to those organisational resources and impaired their own effectiveness. The common learning process that resulted from the confrontation with the allegedly stubborn, rigid Germans led the rather individualistic Frenchmen towards more discipline, organisation and clarity. Their chaotic, vague shadow side was balanced out, but at no cost to their own life style. The Germans learned, through teamwork with the French, to communicate on a more personal basis, to take breaks and really enjoy them, and to remain calm and relaxed when conflicts arose. At the same time, they continued to value their own strengths and still paid attention to facts, deadlines and agreements.

Diagram of a development square using the example of a German-French IT team

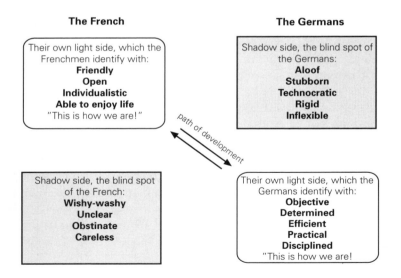

Intercultural relationship management does not mean adapting to all of the habits of others. Rather, it means recognising the attitudes from the other culture that are missing in one's self. These usually turn out to be exactly those qualities that we find so irritating in others.

If we can identify the light side of the "other", we can use this to expand our own awareness and range of behaviours. In the long run, it is a win-win situation. The combination of macro-system constellations and micro-system follow-up creates a good prognosis for joint ventures, mergers and cooperation in the course of internationalism and globalisation.

5.3 THE INVISIBLE POWER SYSTEM IN YOUR PERSONALITY

Every personality is comprised of many personality parts.

"*I am many ,I's*" – Anyone hoping for competence in leadership and communication must recognise this fact. It means that you do not have to decide "once and for all" to make a choice between being submissive or dominating, cooperative or egocentric. You can learn to integrate all the aspects of your personality and use them for effective self-management.

A personality is not a single unit. Every personality consists of many, sometimes contradictory, "sub-personalities", which have been formed in the course of that person's life. The formation of the parts of the personality lies far back in the past.

How it all begins

The first personality parts ensure survival.

Every newborn being is unique. If you've got children, you will certainly be able to confirm this. Every person arrives in the world with a quality of being that makes him or her individual. It has been called the "psychic fingerprint". Besides being unique, the newborn is completely unprotected and vulnerable and hence totally dependent upon the care of others, which usually means the parents. How does a personality form in such a tiny being that allows the person to say later, "*This is who I am. This is how I am. This is my character.*"?

Because the infant cannot take care of itself, it has to develop a way of ensuring that help is forthcoming and the vulnerable being is protected. Therein lie the beginnings of the personality. This "watchdog" has the task of an inner protector/controller. The qualities of these first personality parts may vary, depending on the child's culture and country, and on family circumstances, values and standards. The most important task of the primary selves is to ensure survival at any cost. There are various "helper" parts that develop as further aspects of the personality as the child adapts to the individual circumstances of his or her life. We will look at this development using the case example of Laura and Rolf.

Laura's family

The atmosphere in Laura's family is calm and friendly. As the first born, she is enthusiastically welcomed by her parents. The first "selves" of Laura that assist her inner protection and guard functions develop very different strategies to those of Rolf, whose family lives in a loud and turbulent lifestyle. Rolf, as the third child, also has to share his parents' love and attention with two other siblings. What inner helpers are developed to ensure the survival of these two people?

A baby quickly learns what works.

Laura's parents lovingly devote much time caring for her. She feels mummy and daddy's love particularly strongly when she is lying happily and quietly in her bed and when she smiles at them. But sometimes Laura isn't in the mood to smile; perhaps she is especially hungry or has a tummy ache. She gets whiney and grouchy or even screams loudly. Her mummy comes to pick her up and take care of her, but not quite as lovingly as usual. Laura, tiny as she is, senses this very clearly. She soon recognises that her feelings are not of primary importance here. She learns, *"When I am nice and friendly and pay attention to what others expect of me and what pleases them, then I get what I need."* As an infant, these needs are mother's milk and her parents' love. Later, other kinds of attention from other people are involved. This process occurs automatically and completely unconsciously.

In Laura, an important part of her personality develops to act as "assistant" to her protector/controller function, this inner helper is a "pleaser". *

---

* The term "pleaser" was introduced by Hal and Sidra Stone, the founders of the *Voice Dialogue Method.*

In the "good child", aggressive impulses are pushed aside.

In the course of her life, this inner person in Laura develops very sensitive antennae for what other people need. With her "pleaser" Laura can influence her surroundings in a gentle way – a skill that she makes good use of later. However, what happens to Laura's aggressive side, the part of her that loudly demands her rights? Contrary to the "pleaser", this part is not concerned with accommodating, but rather with asserting herself and getting what she needs. The needs of others are secondary to this part of the personality. This is a development that has later consequences.

Protecting vulnerability takes priority.

In the example of Laura, aggressive behaviour was punished, even though the punishment was very subtle. The consequence of such behaviour was a greater or lesser withholding of love on the part of her parents. Since Laura was totally dependent upon her parents' love, her protector/guard function could not be assisted by aggression and assertion to protect her vulnerability and ensure her survival. These vital energies do not simply evaporate, but they are put away somewhere where they pose no risk to her survival. We will look later at the consequences for Laura and her development.

Rolf's family

When the power type develops, the pleaser is stored away.

Now we turn to Rolf. His family was usually loud and aggressive. Everyday family life was marked by noise from the street, television, the screaming and quarrelling of his siblings, and overwhelmed parents who tended towards emotional outbursts. Although his parents loved him and were pleased when he was a good little boy, Rolf learned very early that, *"If I want something, I have to be loud and assertive in order to be noticed."* He learned as a baby to make himself heard by bellowing long and loudly. That technique was successful; his mum finally heard him and came! This marked the beginning of an important part of his personality, *the power type.* What happened to the part of Rolf that considered others and tried to please them? You have certainly guessed it. Just as Laura's aggressive part was stored away, the same thing happened to Rolf's "pleaser".

We meet our disowned personality parts again in others.

As demands change, through nursery school, school, or through changes in the family, many other inner personality parts develop. These parts of the personality, emerging at different times in different phases in our lives, all have the same task – to protect our vulnerability. Whether we are seven or seventy, that vulnerable child still lives inside of us.

How does the protector/controller, with its assistants, protect that inner child? It simply locks up all of those inner parts that have proven too weak in the past to do the job of protecting. Those parts are disowned and lead a shadow existence.

These parts sometimes make an appearance in our dreams, but the messages from dreams are usually so coded that we cannot understand them. The "banned" personality parts, the disowned selves, remain undisturbed to "leave well enough alone", but that does not always work. Besides their appearance in dreams, these inner persons that have been shunted off to the side make themselves felt when we feel irritated by certain characteristics in another person.

Effects on the adult

We will return to Laura and Rolf. Thirty years later, they are both professionals, and both have a significant other in their lives. Laura has become a warm hearted and well-liked young woman. As we remember, Laura (or her pleaser) had developed a fine sensitivity for whatever helps her to be accepted by others. Consequently people are almost always on her side – except for a new colleague at work.

This woman embodies exactly the qualities that Laura cannot stand in others; she is egocentric and stubborn! As Laura describes the new colleague, *"She comes first, then eventually, a long way down the list, come other people!"* The colleague reacts to Laura's friendliness with condescension. The only way Laura could please this new colleague would be with a power type personality, something that is not available to her. The only way Laura can stand on an equal footing with this new colleague, and others who identify themselves with power, is to find access to that strength in herself. This would allow her to stand up for herself clearly and consistently.

A power type cannot access pleaser qualities.

Rolf has chosen a profession in which he can use the qualities of a "power type" and apply them to ensure his success. At the age of thirty, he has already climbed a good way up the ladder of success. He only has difficulty with people who *"won't say straight out what they want, and who would rather be taken advantage of than speak up for themselves!"* *"Spineless wimps,"* he calls them contemptuously. It would be fine with him to just leave it at that if it weren't for the department he has just taken over.

As luck would have it, there are a few people in this department who fit that description to a T.! In his straightforward, sometimes brusque style, he often runs up against resistance from them. In this situation, he could well use a personality part that accommodates others and focuses on them – an aspect of a pleaser. As we remember, though, this has been pushed aside in Rolf's personality.

Why is it that we are only able to see the shadow side of the personality part that we have banned in ourselves? In Laura's family, her assertive, aggressive side was negatively received and if that side of her came out, her vulnerability was at risk. Because she was unable to develop and experiment with her power side, it is too weak to protect her and it is safer to keep it under lock and key. Laura can do that most effectively by flatly rejecting aggressive behaviour, in herself as well as in others. The same is true for Rolf in the reverse. In his family, he would not have been able to get what he needed using friendliness, so he has to devalue the pleaser in himself and others to secure his own safety.

You stand more securely on two legs.

For a fulfilling and successful life, we need *both* assertive strength and sensitivity. These oppositional capabilities are like two legs that allow us to stand and move securely. When we limit ourselves to what protected our vulnerability at an earlier age, we limp through adult life on one leg. As a children's game, hopping around on one leg is great fun, but as a long-term solution, it is strenuous and unsatisfactory. Therefore we look for another "leg" in our "better half", our life partners, and in friends and business partners.

This external support is comfortable, but leaves us dependent for life and does not help us to develop our own balance. Therefore we have to give up our habit of hobbling around on one leg and learn to stand on two feet. Just as the children who are only playing a hopping game, we always have the missing "leg" at our disposal. The trick is to let it come out and come to life. A first step in this direction is to gain insight into the scope of our complexity and the dynamics at work – a relationship much like a government party in power and the opposition party.*

The inner governing body

Our whole personality is comprised of different parts, or selves, that have various qualities and skills. There are some that are powerful and some that are weak, some loud, others quiet. Some form sub-groups or coalitions with others just as if there were a government in power and an opposition party, and perhaps even a faction of revolutionaries. For example, successful people often have an inner governing body made up of "pushers" and perfectionists. Their motto is *"Get going! Faster, higher, further!" "Just do it!"* When the ruling coalition takes on an assistant that is concerned with satisfying everyone else's needs, there will be no peace until the entire structure has adapted to everyone's satisfaction. As we all know, this is a task for Sisyphus, the poor man condemned by the gods to ceaselessly roll a stone to the top of a mountain, only to have it roll back down again. It guarantees stress!

An inner governing body that demands achievement will not make allowances for relaxation.

The parts of the personality that love to relax and contemplate the enjoyment of life will be denounced as "lazy" and excluded by such a ruling party. From a position of exile, the only path open to these parts for getting their interests represented is a clever sabotage of "government projects". For example when the governing body has decreed that work must be done on holidays, these other parts ensure that the laptop and mobile are accidentally "forgotten" at home in the flurry of leaving. Yet another personality part comes forth to speak at this point, the inner critic. *"How typical! You can't even remember the most important details! You idiot!"*

The inner critic supports the achiever government.

Do you know this critic? He or she also comments on your appearance when you've had a great time at a party and then look in the

---

* We have presented a very simplified, condensed version of the development of personality. For a more complete treatment, see the works of Stone and of Wittemann.

mirror the next morning, or when you step on the scales after holiday excesses. This part often works together with the pusher/perfectionist government and strengthens their power. Even the governing body has to step back sometimes when the situation demands, but that is usually short-lived, as the following example shows.

An example in a work situation

Mr T is head of a department and is a person with such an inner governing body. He has a management problem in that his employees put up a fierce resistance to his leadership style, and others give notice after a brief period of time with him. He does a systemic constellation of the situation in hopes of improving cooperation at work. The constellation shows that the balance of giving and taking is out of alignment. Unconsciously anxious about possibly making too many demands on his employees and driving them away, Mr T takes over everything himself.

In addition, his "perfectionist" personality part insists that he can do it faster and better himself anyway. Without noticing, he refuses to allow or recognise independent performance in his team. This guarantees that the "doer" and the "perfectionist" in him achieve exactly what he would like to prevent – the employees go elsewhere!

The solution pictured in the constellation is for him to step back, from managing to a guiding function, from doing to delegating. Mr T agrees with the solution, but his inner governing body does not. Although he says yes, inner objections arise. *"You will lose too much time! We won't get done in time! You have more experience! Don't put our high standard of quality at risk!"* Since Mr T has never met his inner government, he is not consciously aware of this inner dialogue. He only feels torn in a way that he cannot explain.

The inner governing body is stronger than rational understanding.

Immediately following the constellation, it seems, much to the amazement of his employees, that Mr T has changed his style of management. But, gradually he reverts back to his old role. What has happened? His inner government sat back and watched for a while as other personality parts practiced a completely new style of management, one that could delegate, which was not normally a skill Mr

T had at his disposal. Soon, the "pusher/perfectionist" party deemed it too risky and took back the reins. *"End of experiment!"* was declared and the old, time-tested practice was reinstated.

In this case, the systemic resolution in the work relationship can only function if Mr T gets macro-micro-coaching to give him some room to move. The solution does not depend on the macro-system of the company, but on the micro-system of his personality structure, or of his family system.

Macro-micro-coaching uses a practical technique from humanistic psychology called "Voice Dialogue", * which allows individuals to become aware of conflicts within themselves or with others and helps to resolve them. The coach speaks with the personality parts involved in the conflict, as if speaking to real, complete people.

The coach speaks to the inner persons.

Through listening and treating the opposing parts with serious respect, the parts can be brought into a harmonious relationship and aligned in a proper balance. As you have probably guessed, the inner people – multiple I's – behave just as people in a family or work system such as a team. That is why the personality system is referred to as an "inner team" (Schulz von Thun) or an "inner family" (Schwartz). As all human systems, the personality system functions according to certain principles or rules that protect and stabilise it and allow for continuing development.

In our experience, these laws essentially correspond to the principles that keep interpersonal systems together and functioning. Although it is not a complete picture, we will present some of the systemic principles presented in Chapter 1, in the context of effects on the micro-system of the personality.

What is must be allowed to be.

Some of our inner "persons" express themselves in ways that we do not like very much. "We", in this case, means our inner governing body. Even in a self-confident, active, decisive person, for example, there is a shy, hesitant voice. This part must be allowed to be there. If permission is denied for this voice to exist, conflict is inevitable. If

---

*   This method was developed by Hal and Sidra Stone: Embracing Ourselves, San Francisco

the voice is respected, it can make a contribution to the whole – perhaps in situations that call for sensitivity and reserve.

A balance of giving and taking
When the doers and perfectionists demand a lion's share of the time available, there is little left over for the connoisseur or the pleasure-lover within us. Long-term, it does not work out well, as symptoms of excess stress and psychosomatic illness are often the costs of such an imbalance. The solution is the same; consciously arrange a better balance between the opposing parts.

The right to belong
In the entire personality, every inner person has a particular history and exists for a particular reason. Therefore each must have the right to speak and to contribute something to the whole personality. If this right is denied by the stronger personality parts, the weaker parts go underground. Like freedom fighters, these banned and denied inner persons know how to make themselves heard through effectively sabotaging projects of those in power. These acts of sabotage are of various kinds. One variation is the appearance of stress-related, psychosomatic illness; inexplicable runs of bad luck and failure are another. The exiled parts can become resources when they are made conscious and given a place and recognition in the inner system.

Priority ranking for those who came first over those who came later
The personality parts that were developed first are those that ensured our survival in childhood. In a micro-system constellation, it is often apparent that these primary selves play a more central role than those inner persons that were developed later. This priority ranking has to be respected by powerful inner persons that arrive later. The situation is exactly the same as a new manager coming into a firm, who has to lead from the last position. This means that a person like Laura, who is "pleaser" dominant, will only be able to use a power side if she has the friendly intervention of the pleaser. She will always have a steel fist gloved in velvet. If she were to attempt to change drastically and develop a radical power stance like Rolf's, she would throw out the baby with the bathwater and would surely fail. Her pleaser would just find a clever way to weaken the power voice in order to make its own presence felt again.

Priority to parts that contribute more essentially to the whole

The parts of the inner team that are essentially important for survival at the present moment have more power and influence than those team members responsible for lower priorities. For example, an engineer who has always wanted to be a musician will feel an inner conflict and life-long dissatisfaction. The artistic opposition rebels continuously against the rational, technical governing body and declares the government's goals to be boring or petty. The resolution would be for the artistic personality parts to acknowledge that the technical practical side is responsible for the basic needs of living. That would mean accepting second place in the inner system, giving up hopes of overturning the government, and ceasing to undermine the work of the governing body.

In everyday life our engineer would have more energy for work and could more effectively devise a plan that would satisfy the music in his veins. He would be able to consciously make time for his music, the time that his inner opposition has had to steal or secretly slip in.

In the chart below, we present an overview of the consequences that arise when these systemic principles are violated.

5.4 MANAGING YOUR INNER TEAM

Now that you are acquainted with the invisible power structure of the personality system, we invite you to take the next step – the practical management of your inner team. We will present two different case studies to illuminate this step. In the first section, you will see how the constellation method can be applied to the inner team. The second section details the use of the *voice dialogue* method to work with relationship patterns and inner opposites. In both cases we have summarised the most important steps of the coaching sessions. The personal details of our clients have been changed to protect their privacy and any similarity to actual persons or organisations is purely coincidental.

The Invisible Power Structure of the Personality

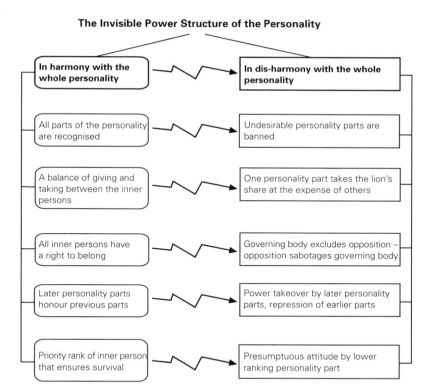

In harmony with the whole personality	In dis-harmony with the whole personality
All parts of the personality are recognised	Undesirable personality parts are banned
A balance of giving and taking between the inner persons	One personality part takes the lion's share at the expense of others
All inner persons have a right to belong	Governing body excludes opposition – opposition sabotages governing body
Later personality parts honour previous parts	Power takeover by later personality parts, repression of earlier parts
Priority rank of inner person that ensures survival	Presumptuous attitude by lower ranking personality part

Assisting work-related decision with a micro-system constellation

Background information

Mr L comes to us for a personal coaching session for help with a professional decision that is very important to him. He describes the background of the issue.

Mr L is married and has two children. For the past few years, he has been department head in a medium-sized business in a rural area. Recently he has had the feeling that he is just running in place because there are no new challenges or opportunities for personal growth. There is no room in this company for professional advancement, as he already reports directly to the owner / director. He does not want to see this as the end point of his career, so he has begun to check out opportunities in the market. He has received a number of interesting offers, but decided against each one for various reasons. Each time he has turned down a job he has been worried by a feeling of having passed up a chance.

Missing a chance?

Mr L: Now I've got a new offer from an international company. From our initial meetings, it would seem that I'm the perfect person for the job. The people I've talked to there think the same. In this company I would have all the opportunities for development that I want. But even though the offer is very attractive, I am still hesitating and can't make a decision. In the meantime there is an on-going discussion with my wife, who can't understand what's going on.

His reasons for turning down job offers appear increasingly incomprehensible to him and seem to be more like pretexts. But why? This is the issue he would like to explore in coaching. As he says, *"I'm running out of time."*

Coach: As you present it, it seems as if two very different forces are at work within you. One part wants to accept the challenge and is ready for a career leap and another voice inside you makes you hesitate and then turn it down. We can assume that this part considers security to be of utmost importance.

Mr L: Yes, exactly. The job I have is safe. I could sit in this position until I retire. But I notice that when I mention that prospect, my stomach turns over.

Coach: So this other part makes an entrance on stage?

Mr L: Right! It goes back and forth like that.

Coach: Okay. I would suggest we begin with a micro-system constellation. That means we will set up the parts of the personality that we presume are involved. Then we can look at these forces that are working in different directions and see how they stand in relation to you. We can also find out what this battle is about and perhaps find a solution. Are you prepared to do that?

Mr L: Yes, okay.

Coach: Although we know what you're interested in exploring, it is still important to formulate the issue very precisely. What exactly is your goal? What do you want to achieve with this constellation?

The issue

The coach helps Mr L with the formulation of his issue, until he is able to state it precisely.

Mr L: My goal is to get an inner "green light" for this important career move. I would also like to know what is holding me back.

Coach: Assuming we were successful today, how exactly would you know it?

Mr L: This inner pressure would be gone. Perhaps I would also be able to look at this new tempting alternative more rationally and weigh the pros and cons. Then I could either go for it or look elsewhere with a clear sense of what I am looking for.
Coach: Good, let's begin with the constellation!

When we are in an individual session and have no representatives to be used in the constellation, we utilise other materials. In this case we use cardboard squares of various colours to symbolise the positions. The squares are large enough for a person to stand on comfortably, and notches in one side indicate the direction the person is facing. Either the client stands on the cardboard squares, or the coach takes over the various roles. In all other respects the procedure is similar to a constellation with representatives.

Coach: What would you like to call that part of your personality that favours a career change?
Mr L: That part is someone looking at the other side of the river and ready to take a risk.
Coach: So this is someone who does not hesitate for long, but gets right to it?
Mr L: Yes, a doer!
Coach: Good. Shall we call him "Doer"? (Mr L agrees) What do you want to call his counterpart? How about "Security Caretaker"?
Mr L: Yes, that fits.

The constellation
Mr L chooses a cardboard square for:

- *Him, Himself*
- *The Doer*
- *The Security Caretaker* (in the constellation called "security")
- *The Current Company,* in which Mr L is department head
- *The Potential New Company,* with a chance for advancement, in the constellation called "new company"

Coach: Position each of the five cardboard squares, one after another, according to your inner sense of their relationship to one another. Pay attention to the notched side that symbolises the direction it is facing. Begin with your own square, and then place the "doer", and "security". Ask yourself exactly where in the room these two parts of your personality would be if they were not inside you? Lay them out in relation to the square that represents you. Then position the other two squares, the current company and the new company, in relationship to the others.

Mr L's issue invites a combination of the macro- and micro-systems in the constellation. That means that parts of the personality as well as persons or institutions involved in the issue are set up in the constellation.

When he has marked the positions on the floor using the coloured squares, we look at the configuration together.

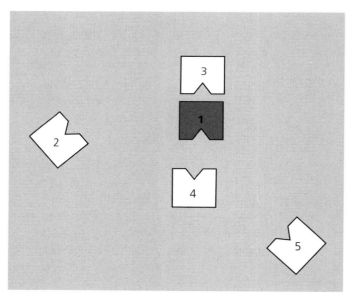

1	Mr L	4	Current company, in which
2	Inner "oder"		Mr L is department head
3	Inner security caretaker	5	Potential new company

Fig. 1: Situation as it is

Coach: Does anything stand out for you when you look at this image?
Mr L: Someone is breathing down the back of my neck. At least that's the way it looks.

Coach: We can check that out. Stand on the square that you have laid out to represent you. Take some time to get tuned into this place.

Mr L

When Mr L has stood in this place for a while, his posture and facial expression begin to change.

Coach: How do you feel there?

Mr L: Tense, and my shoulders are tight! There really is something breathing down my neck! This is very uncomfortable! Who is that square behind me again?

Coach: The part of you that considers security important. What else are you aware of in relation to the other positions?

Mr L: I can only see what is to the right and to the left out of the corner of my eye. It's almost as if I'm not allowed to look there, as if I would be guilty of something.

Coach: Against someone?

Mr L: That I can't say. In any case, the longer I stand wedged in here between these two (indicates security and the current company), the more uptight I feel.

The doer

The coach now asks Mr L to leave that position, walk around the room a bit, and then stand on the square that represents his inner doer.

Coach: How are things with the part of Mr L that goes after things?

The coach helps Mr L to activate his inner doer and give it a voice, by connecting to a similar personality part in himself. His own tone of voice also changes and becomes more demanding and insistent.

Doer: Well, in this position I don't have any impact. I can try to persuade him all I want. He (indicates the square representing Mr L) can't even see me here! Out of the corner of his eye? What does he think? That life is there so you can look at the really important things out of the corner of your eye?

Coach: You're pretty angry with him! If it were up to you, what do you think he ought to do in regard to his issue? What would you advise him?

Doer: It's perfectly clear. Take it! Take it! How many offers does he need in order to get it? The competitors aren't asleep. He thinks he's still got plenty of time. He hasn't got a clue, this dreamer! Soon, he's going to be out of the picture.

Coach: That was clearly stated. Have you got any sense of the others? How do you feel about security, for example, that Mr L put behind himself?

Doer: When I look over there, I feel sick! How is he going to move forwards when he's got this security caretaker breathing down his neck and the company in front of him? Jammed in with security! No one has ever made a career that way! With that hanging on his neck, he'll let the next ten offers float out the window, guaranteed! He boycotts every move forwards!

Coach: Thank you for this very informative discussion.

Mr L

The coach asks Mr L to leave the position of the doer and return to his own position. Mr L seems a bit more relaxed. The coach asks him how he feels now.

Mr L: Was that me? I can hardly believe that I let loose with that tirade. I don't know that side of me at all!

Coach: Yes this part of you is rather angry but also worried about you. In everyday life, we are not usually very aware of this voice. We often feel the anger only in external symptoms such as tension, stomach problems, and so on.

As you may have noticed, an uninvited guest has shown up to take part in the discussion – the inner critic. In this case, that part has allied himself with the "doer".

Security

Coach: Now let's hear what the other side (indicates security) has to say about the situation. Are you ready?

Mr L leaves his position, walks around the room a bit to prepare himself for a different energy, and then, he stands in the position of security. Before the coach speaks with this new personality part in Mr L, he makes contact with his own inner security caretaker, to support him in activating and holding the energy of this part of the personality.

Coach: How is it for the part of Mr L who feels security is very important?

When he has stood on this place for a while, his body posture changes. The large, imposing man now seems much smaller.

Security (in a quiet, serious voice): I don't feel well here. This is much too tight for me! What am I doing behind him? I don't want to breathe down his neck. That's ridiculous!
Coach: If you don't want to be breathing down his neck, where would be a better place for you?
Security: Over there (indicates the place next to the current company). We belong together. That's where his future is. From there he can look into the future with a good feeling about himself and for his family!
Coach: Well, you've heard that he isn't happy with the way his professional prospects look for the future. What is your concern? What are you worried about and what are you trying to protect him from?
Security: I only want what's best for him!
Coach: But the doer said the same thing.
Security: That over there (points to the new company square) is nothing but a fantasy. He gets bonus pay where he works now! What if it doesn't work out? What if he can't manage that leap and he fails? Nobody would ever take him seriously again. Word gets around. Then what happens to his wife and children? Two children, that costs a lot! Now they're still small, but what about later? How is he going to pay to educate two children? And even if he were to make it, at what price? He already has no spare time!
Coach: You have a very clear image of what is good for him, that much is clear. Is there anything that could make you alter your position? Something that Mr L could do that would make you feel less strongly about this issue?
Security: No! He should just give up this rubbish about career and listen to me. Then I'll feel less strongly. Then, he won't feel me breathing down his neck any more. I'm sure you've heard the expression, "The bigger they are, the harder they fall!" That's my opinion and

I've got nothing more to add.

Coach: Thank you for speaking with me.

The coach asks Mr L to leave this position and return to the square that represents him.

Mr L was very quickly able to establish contact with his personality parts and give them a voice but does not always happen that quickly. Sometimes a longer warm-up period is needed before the inner voices are prepared to give their view of the situation.

Coach: You have grown again!

Mr L (having a good stretch): In that position (indicates security) I felt as if I was wearing a suit that was too small.

Coach: Does that expression sound familiar to you? "The bigger they are, the harder they fall"?

Mr L: Yes, I've been thinking about that the whole time. To be honest, everything that I said there (indicates the security square) sounds familiar to me. Only, it belongs to someone else. (He is suddenly very thoughtful).

The father

Coach: Who are you thinking about?

Mr L: That's almost word for word from my father! That expression you asked about was something I heard all throughout my childhood and adolescence.

Coach: It seems that we have ended up at an important point for you. Tell me something about him. Is your father still alive?

Mr L: Yes. My father has always been a very important person to me. He wasn't just a rigid value system that I often fought against; he was always there for me when I needed him. My mother always had the new ideas and projects in mind. She was never satisfied with the way things were. My father used to joke that she was the motor and he was the brake. And what a brake! That was the side of him that I absolutely could not stand. No experiments! He never got any further that his one little post in his job. In my protest phase I always made fun of him because he was satisfied all those years with the same job and the same old car. I can still hear him saying, "Let it be, lad. Here I know what I've got. The air is too thin up there for me."

It's exactly how I did not want to become!

Coach: Yes, I see. Except that is practically a guarantee that exactly that is what will turn up!

Mr L: That's hard to accept!

Coach: I believe you. In adolescence it is very important to separate yourself from your parents. We believe that in doing that we can leave them, their way of thinking and their values, and go our own way and do things differently, perhaps even better. The only problem is that it doesn't work that way. Instead, we remain unconsciously dependent upon them for our entire lives and although we don't want to do it, we repeat everything that we disapproved of in them, even long after they are dead. What we can do to separate from our parents on the inside is very practical and actually pretty unspectacular. We can acknowledge and honour our parents, exactly as they are. If you're ready, we'll continue with that.

Mr L agrees. The coach takes an additional square of cardboard and asks Mr L to place it at some distance from his own square, so that they are facing each other. Mr L returns to the square that represents him. From there he can easily see the new position.

Coach: Imagine that this new square represents your father. Can you get an image of your father?

Mr L nods after a while.

Coach: Look at your father. Can you still see him? (nod) How is your father looking at you?

Mr L: Worried.

Coach: What do you call your father?

Mr L: Father.

Coach: Look at him and tell him, "Father, I am exactly like you. I am following in your footsteps. Because you couldn't make much out of your career, I won't, either.

After some hesitation, he repeats the words.

Coach: How was that?

Mr L (shaking his head): I get what you mean. That part of me lives exactly according to his values (indicates square for security). Still, it's the same as when we started this session; it really turns my stomach!

Coach: It looks as if, out of love for your father, you are unconsciously living out his values. He represents that in you (indicates security). If it weren't for him (indicates doer) you wouldn't have a problem. Now you've seen a few things here. The next step will be to consciously release some of this loyalty to your father so that you can get a better balance between these two forces. Look at the place that represents your father; look at him and tell him, "Father, how you live your life is your business. I won't interfere with that any more. I was a bit presumptuous and I'll let that go now."

Mr L repeats these words.

Coach: How is that?

Mr L: That was a relief. It's as if somebody has taken a weight off my shoulders!

Coach: Now say to him, "Father, please be friendly towards me when I am successful in my work and when I live my life the way I see fit."

When he has repeated these sentences Mr L exhales deeply and smiles.

Coach: You look very different!

Mr L: I can hardly believe what an impact such a simple sentence can have! How can anybody explain that?

Coach: Is there anything else you would like to say to your father?

Mr L: No, that's fine as it is.

With Mr L's help, the coach moves the squares into an image of resolution.

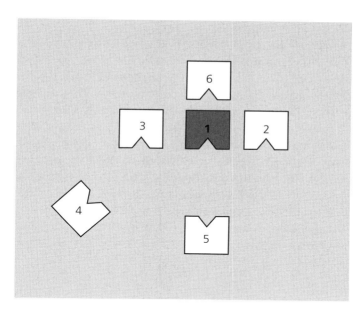

1 Mr L
2 Inner "Doer"
3 Inner Security Caretaker
4 Current Company, in which
   Mr L is department head

5 Potential New Company
6 Mr L's Father

Fig. 2: Image of resolution

Mr L has his *Doer* to his left at about the same distance as *Security* to his right. The *New Company* is in front of him, visible to everyone. The *Current Company* is acknowledged with a place to the side that is also visible to everyone. The *Father's* place is behind his son. Mr L feels this is the best place. *"Very supportive,"* is how he describes the feeling. Finally, the coach has Mr L stand on his own square, look to his right at *Security* and say to him, *"You are the part of me that is most closely connected to my father. Whenever security is important in my life, I will listen to your opinion."* Then, he turns to the left to the *Doer* and says, *"You're the one who moves me forward. If I want to get there* (indicates the *New Company*), *I will really need you."* In the final step, Mr L stands once again at each of the positions of his personality parts and notices the differences in his awareness in each place. The constellation ends.

After a few weeks we get a phone call from Mr L. and we are curious to know what he has decided. *"It couldn't be better,"* he tells us. He feels he was right on the mark in having the coaching session at exactly the right time. He has decided not to take the job, and when we ask him why, he replies, *"That job would have been like an ejector seat!"* We ask how he got clear about that. He explains that he didn't get clear about it. His "security caretaker" is responsible for that clarity, and since our session Mr L has often asked this part for advice. He unearthed more information about the job and, as petty as this part is, he looked at all the small print. Even the doer part couldn't find anything to add that would balance it out. *"Everything else I learned from you. The next job interview is already scheduled! But I'm not under so much pressure any more, and for the first time I have the feeling that I have a real choice."*

Expanding alternatives using *voice dialogue*

You are already acquainted with the business consultant, Ms M, from her supervision constellation in Chapter 3.5. When it became clear from the macro-system constellation that Ms M was being strongly influenced by something from her mother's side, we invited her to work on this imbalance in a session using the *voice-dialogue* method. First, we look at the relationship pattern between Ms M and the future chairman of the board of directors (you met him as the "new boss" in Chapter 3.5, the designated successor to the top job in the bank).

Initially, the consulting sessions with Ms M, the current director and his designated successor went very smoothly and were productive. Danger was lurking in the background, however, because it was not Ms M, but the "good mother" part of her that was able to establish a trusting environment through tireless effort and a friendly approach. The motherly side of Ms M prompts a spontaneous feeling of trust, particularly in men, because she communicates in a very personal way. She is open and warm-hearted, and puts the needs of others first, listening with a fine-tuned ear for any worries or wishes. The more her clients enjoy meeting in such a warm atmosphere, the more inappropriate they find the dominance of this "good mother" when the atmosphere changes in the consulting sessions.

Relationship patterns allow us no choice.

In such situations, Ms M has no access to her impersonal ,business-woman' that has a clear sense of boundaries. She is therefore extremely vulnerable and open to attack when her previously accepted behaviour is suddenly rejected. Along with the inner adult parts that determine our actions, there is also still a vulnerable child side. When we feel hurt, left out or rejected, the reactions we feel come from that side.

We work with Ms M first on the positive relationship pattern between her and Mr K, and then on the switch into the negative. In relationship patterns, it is clear that we are continuously communicating with one another at two levels, the adult level and the level of the child.* In positive relationship patterns, the caring good mother in Ms M looks after the grateful son in Mr K with attention and care. In this harmonious phase of their communication, the benevolent father in Mr K praises the performance of the daughter side in Ms M, and everyone is happy.

Positives: Relationship pattern in the example of Ms M and Mr K

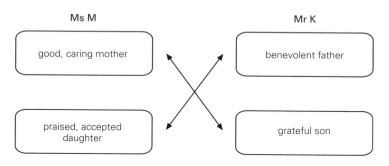

The swing from positive to negative in relationship patterns is unavoidable.

After a while this communication pattern flips into the negative. This is inevitable in any relationship, regardless whether it has to do with a work relationship or a personal one. After the honeymoon comes everyday life with its demands and difficulties. A lasting relation-

---

* For more information about relationship patterns, see the works of Stone.

ship soon swings back to a positive pattern and the partners gradually get used to "seasonal changes". In a relationship with business clients such as this consultant and bank director, that can hardly be expected to happen. The business relationship normally comes to an end and the two move in different directions. Why is there such a pendulum swing in relationship patterns and what triggers it? Looked at systemically, there is not one trigger, no chain of cause and effect, but a simultaneous, circular event.

The change into a negative pattern is often a shock.

Human systems function in a network of reciprocal effects. Any change at one point is immediately felt in the whole network. The vacuum of authority that occurred when the old boss pulled back had a strong pull on the "good mother" in Ms M. She felt needed and leapt into the gap immediately. The more Ms M slipped unconsciously into the role of the secret boss, the more her image changed in Mr K from *good, caring mother* to *controlling, powerful mother.*

Many boys react to such a motherly behaviour with rebellion and stubbornness. It is understandable that Mr K – that is, the boy inside him – reacted in this phase of the consulting with an adolescent nonchalance, provoking Ms M with his condescension. In other words the responsible, reliable banker retreated, leaving in his place a protesting 14-year-old with only one goal – to get out of mother's clutches. The child in Ms M, whose existence is just as unconscious as Mr K's teenager, senses the critical father side of Mr K behind his adolescent acting out.

Her inner child experiences this harsh criticism like a bucket of ice water. Instead of continuing confirmation and acceptance, the child in Ms M is now rebuffed.

Power struggles in the macro-system (in this case the bank and consultant) and an imbalance in the micro-system (personalities) determine one another. Here too it is not enough to ask what came first. The tension in the macro-system could be resolved in the constellation but to help Ms M avoid falling back into the old, unconscious behaviour patterns, or falling into a similar trap in the next consulting situation, she needs to understand the relationship pattern (see chart) and learn to manage the inner parts of her personality more effectively.

Negatives: Relationship pattern in the example of Ms M and Mr K

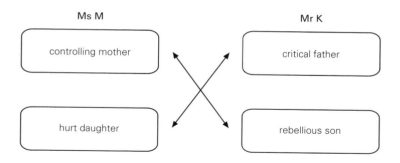

Coaching session with Ms M

To conclude we have a follow-up discussion with Ms M.

Ms M: I understand how this relationship pattern happens and I can see that the mother role keeps getting out of control. But how do I reduce that dominance?

Coach: First, by acknowledging and respecting the good mother and then finding out what other parts of you could also take over in this situation.

Ms M: Well okay, but how does that function in practice? I only noticed after the fact that the good mother was running things!

Coach: Who in you is speaking when you function in a more businesslike and impersonal way?

Ms M: Yes, there is that side of me – I can feel it when I'm dealing with fees – a businesswoman, I would call it.

Coach: Do you notice when this businesswoman takes over the controls?

Ms M: Well actually not, at least not in the moment. As I think about it, it's clear afterwards that she was conducting the business.

Coach: I would suggest that we let the two of them have their say. While I talk with them, you can listen in and very consciously find out what they have to say. Perhaps that will help you to more quickly become aware of who is talking inside you.

Ms M (laughing): Interesting idea! But how does it work for you to talk to them and I listen in?

Coach: Very simply. Which one would you like to begin with?

Ms M (after thinking it over for a moment): I think with the good mother.

Coach: Okay. You already know how to find a place for representatives in a constellation. Do exactly the same thing now. Imagine that this good mother is not inside you, but here in the room. She is a part of your personality so she is always present. Get a sense of where she is in relation to you in the room and take that place.

Ms M stands up, moves a few steps to the side and looks at her own chair. The she moves in the direction of her own place and remains standing to the left, behind her own chair. Her body posture and her facial expression begin to change slightly. It is a process similar to what you see in a constellation when the representatives are placed and feel their way into their roles. The coach asks her if he could speak with the good mother. She says yes and begins to smile at the coach with a friendly, warm-hearted expression.

The good mother

Coach: Hello. It's nice to see you here. Would you like to sit down?

Good Mother: No, thank you, I'm happy to stand.

Coach: You don't seem to be very demanding.

Good Mother: I don't worry much about my own comfort. I'm happy when I can be of service. What can I do for you?

Coach: I would just like to get to know you and I'd like to hear your opinion on a few things that are bothering Ms M. Perhaps it would be helpful for her to hear what you think.

Good Mother: Of course! I worry about her sometimes, most of all when she is too hard in these business things. That only rebounds on you! She should have more understanding for people; after all, she is a consultant. She should take care of her customers and be there for them!

Coach: You're worried that if her "businesswoman" is in control, people won't like her?

Good Mother: She is awfully cool and reserved then. She almost never smiles. In her profession she has to talk to a lot of managers and business leaders. They don't like it when a woman acts like that!

Coach: When you are there, you make sure that Ms M is warmer and more in contact.

Good Mother: Yes, of course! Even leaders of business and industry feel better when they are spoken to in a friendly way. I am happy to take care of her clients' needs and I'm pleased when I can help them to clear up a few problems.

Coach: How was that for you in the bank, when Ms M was advising the two directors?

Good Mother: I was really involved there. I thought it was important that she put in a lot of effort. I think actually that it's a good thing if her clients feel that she wants to help. I was able to take over there and she came out well, I think. Only Mr K gave us some problems. We have to help him to see that he is in a responsible position. After all this concerns the whole firm, not just his personal preferences! I won't leave him and the old boss alone though. We'll get that back under control!

Coach: It seems that he reacts badly to your caretaking though.

Good Mother (smiling)**:** You can't take that too seriously. You know, that's how men are sometimes. Instead of accepting help, they want to prove that they can do it alone. He (Mr K) doesn't even notice how much he is hurting himself and the firm with his behaviour. But as I said, I'll keep supporting him and standing by him until he gets hold of himself again.

Coach: I understand better now what is important to you. It was very informative talking to you. Thank you very much.

The coach asks Ms M to leave the role of the good mother and return to her own place. As she sits down, her facial expression changes and she answers in her normal voice when the coach asks her about her experience as the good mother.

Ms M

Ms M: It is unbelievable, how much the energy from this part of me just runs over people. I have never noticed that before! I can really understand why Mr K would protect himself against that.

Coach: Leaving people a lot of room is not one of the good mother's strong points. But, she has valuable qualities.

Ms M: Yes, I can see that too. I can still feel the strength of this giving quality.

Coach: In the future, you can check out whether her special qualities are useful in a situation or not. If not, let a different member of your team take over, for example your "businesswoman". How about it, can we talk with her as well?

Ms M agrees and proceeds in the same way to find a place for her businesswoman. When she has found a place, she sits up very straight in the chair and crosses her legs in a self-confident manner. She radiates elegance and competence as she looks at the coach and appears friendly and attentive.

The businesswoman

Coach: Good afternoon. Thank you for taking time for this talk.

Businesswoman: I'm happy to do it. It's in my best interest to clear up this situation.

Coach: Good! Let's get right to the point. What was your experience of the situation at the bank and how would you evaluate the situation as it is now?

Businesswoman: That situation spun dangerously out of control. It is not only the question of the transfer of power in the bank that is at stake here, but also my good reputation as a consultant. This project could make or break me! If I had had a say in the matter, I would have stopped that inappropriate interference from her (indicates the position of the good mother). Unfortunately, I wasn't asked.

Coach: You have a good eye for the personal level in consultation.

Businesswoman: That's my job. I make very exact analyses of the network of relationships in my client companies. The ability to put yourself in the right position is just as important for a consultant as practical skills. By the way, I got some valuable input from the systemic constellation in your seminar. It is clear that Mr K had to defend himself against that secret power play. After all, his job is at stake.

Coach: You identify and see through power plays immediately.

Businesswoman: Yes and I also know where my place with my clients is – outside the system. The only way I can advise with objectivity is from a distance. Otherwise I could just as well put myself in as manager and get elected to the board of directors.

Coach: Where you would probably also be successful.

Businesswoman: That may be. But that wouldn't be my kind of thing at all. I prefer more distance and more room to move. I get that more easily in a consulting position than in a leadership position. Never mind the fact that I personally know of no bank that would have a woman on the board of directors.

The coach has Ms M leave the position of the businesswoman and return to her own place. When she has taken her seat, he asks for her impressions.

Ms M
Ms M (thoughtfully): Yes, if I always had her (indicates the chair of the businesswoman) competence at hand when I needed it, it would be great. But I don't.
Coach: When do you particularly need her?
Ms M: When conflicts slide into the level of relationships in a client company and what is needed is a clear delineation between the level of relationships and the level of factual information. Like what happened at the bank.
Coach: What happened instead?
Ms M: The need to help at all costs, to get in there and do something. That quality just rushed in automatically, this "good mother" part.
Coach: You have just seen that you are not only the good mother. She is only a part of your personality, just like the businesswoman and numerous other inner persons. Are you aware of the good mother from where you are sitting now? (She nods.) Good. Invite her to fill up your space with her energy. Imagine you have a dial like the one on your stereo that you can use to turn that energy up or down. (Ms M nods.) Okay, now turn up the good mother energy, but only to the point where there is still enough room for you to still be there.

Ms M tunes in to this part of her personality in the way described. After a short while, her expression and body posture change as we saw earlier in the discussion with the good mother.

Coach: She's there now. Can you feel her?

Ms M smiles and nods her head. She takes a few minutes to sense the presence of this personality part.

Coach: Okay, now turn her energy back down again until you are just barely aware of her, but at a distance.

This process takes a bit longer, and it clearly takes some effort for Ms M to persuade her guest to leave. Finally she succeeds, as reflected in her expression and body language.

Coach: Ah, you've done it!

Ms M (taking a deep breath): Yes, that wasn't so easy. She is very persistent!

Coach: Oh yes, she has an enormous amount of energy. But you have just seen that you can manage it. You can decide when she is invited and when she is to leave. Who is in charge here?

Ms M (hesitates): Yeah, me?

Coach: Exactly, you! You are the head of the team and the good mother is a member of your inner team. She is a valuable and important team member. If you continue to hone your skills as a team leader she will not come in uninvited, but she will consult with you about her contribution. You decide who you need in any given situation. If it's the good mother, ask her to participate just as you have done here, and give her a job. Arrange a signal with her, a pre-programmed number. But when you need the businesswoman, leave the good mother on the reserve bench and send her competent, business-savvy colleague on to the field.

Ms M: I can't quite imagine doing that with the businesswoman. Does that work the same way?

Coach: Try it out.

As described above, Ms M allows the businesswoman part of her to fill her own body and discovers that she can invite her in and also ask her to leave. As with the good mother, she arranges certain signals that she can use to activate and de-activate this inner person. Finally, Ms M practices activating both inner personalities at the same time and then de-activating them, so that she can mix their qualities in everyday situations as needed. She manages to do this as well.

Activating inner persons

Coach: You have taken an important step. In relation to your good mother and your businesswoman you have developed a more aware ego. At this point you can be aware of both of them without one taking over control automatically. Because you were present as an aware ego, you were able to stand between the two factions and have a choice of either. At the same time, you can feel the attraction towards just letting one of the two take over. In everyday life, it is initially not very easy to resist that pull, but in time you will become stronger as the head of your inner team. It also is a help coincidentally in developing your outer leadership qualities. There too it is important not to unconsciously give preference to one employee to the detriment of others, but to keep them all in mind, each with their own unique qualities. You can then decide with clarity and certainty which one is best for which job.

At this point the coaching session is ended with a final transfer exercise. Ms M continues the coaching process until she has reached her goal and has access to new alternatives.

5.5 Training the head of the inner team – An aware ego in everyday life

Systemic solutions are not final. Human systems are in a constant state of flux so there is no "once and for all" solution. As the ancient Greek philosopher Heraclitus said, "you cannot step twice into the same river." This is true of the micro-system of the personality as well as the macro-systems in which we participate (family, business nation, culture, and so on). Although we cannot stop the flow of life, people have always searched for a calm place to stand, outside the rush of everyday reality, from which they can look at and influence things in a clear and relaxed way.

In the flow of life instead of outside it

When it comes to observation and insight, some people are able to find a neutral observer position through meditation, or in the abstract. In business-orientated systems however, observation and insight are not enough; we need to act. For this we have to abandon our panoramic view and step into the stream of everyday life, with all its whirlpools and currents. We are immediately confronted with the oppositional forces that determine us, and clear vision quickly evaporates. One inner voice says one thing and another demands the opposite. Colleagues want to persuade you to go for option A, your boss wants option B, and your client wonders what is wrong with option C. To keep your perceptions and actions clear and conscious, you need a flexible base of awareness in yourself. You need a strong and conscious ego that is prepared to take action. You need to be able to deal with the various inner and outer influences that are reacting to you and to make clear decisions. This conscious "I" develops gradually as you work free of the influence of your inner governing body and its counterparts.

An aware ego can be developed in everyday conflicts.

Before we go on to examples of the working mode of an aware ego, we need to clarify one important fact. No one can "own" a conscious ego. It is not something that suddenly appears and remains forever. It is not a skill like driving a car. It is a process that demands a continual, conscious effort.

In a concrete situation, your aware ego grows out of the opposing demands on you from without and within.

How do you know when you are in this mode of awareness? You know because you have a choice between A and B, when previously you would have automatically said A. For example, an employee asks for a day off, and the "nice boss" in you immediately wants to grant that wish. At the same time, you might hear another, more egocentric voice that says, *"Don't do it! Otherwise, you will have to worry about who is going take over that work!"* If you do not automatically follow the "nice" or the "egocentric" voice, but take both seriously into consideration, a more aware "I" exists for a moment in this situation. You can see very practically that being egocentric is not good; being "nice" is not good; but having a choice is good!

A more conscious "I" gives you more room to move.

Whatever you decide to do in the actual situation, you have listened to both sides and will be able to stand by your decision. Whereas before, you would have heard the criticism of the inner person who was not chosen (*"You inconsiderate egotist!" "What a wimp!", and so on*), you are now at one with yourself.

An aware ego recognises and moderates the different selves before a decision is made, just as a good team leader does with all the members of the team. Your inner team boss can stand between the opposites, for example, between the firm stance of the voice of reason and the feelings of an inner helper.

In this way you come to know that you are not just nice and friendly, but also not just sensible and practical. You have both at your disposal and can draw upon each in the amount called for in the situation. You have a choice and you know immediately that you are not the sensible person you may have thought you were. You see your sensible side as a part of your self. In relation to this part of your personality, your "I" is more conscious and aware and can observe the pros and cons of the voice of reason.

190

With the help of your coach, perhaps you will discover further parts of your personality; perhaps there is a carefree, freedom-loving voice that is sitting in the corner, frustrated because the sensible voice is in complete control. That voice probably can only be heard when it sabotages the projects of the sensible one. The aware ego can stand between the opposing influences of the practical side and the free-wheeling side without automatically following either. It can weigh things. New options develop for a person who was previously in the grip of a controlling personality part and believed, *"This is the way I am. I can't change."* That may have been true, but that "I" wasn't the real "I".

Developing your personality does not mean finally getting everything under control, once and for all. It means managing your inner team in a responsible way.

Difficult people bring not only trouble, but also a gift.

Assume, for example, that you have to work with a person who is very difficult for you. You experience his behaviour as arrogant and high-handed and consider him incompetent as well. When you are giving a presentation in meetings, he is always breaking in with his unfounded objections and doesn't even seem to notice how much he gets on your nerves, or how disruptive his behaviour is. If you are under the influence of your inner governing body that is working for understanding, cooperation and friendliness, you will try to understand him. You remember your communications training and try active listening,: *"You are not completely in agreement with my approach, Mr Y."* But that doesn't seem to have any effect, so you send him a friendly but clear I-message, *"Mr Y, you have just interrupted my presentation for the third time. I find that very disruptive! I would like to ask you to hold your questions until I have finished!"* Your colleague takes note of this, but after a short while he continues as before. Slowly but surely you build towards a crisis.

Inside yourself, you hear from a confrontational, angry voice that would like to overthrow your inner governing body and begin arming for battle. *"Let me at him!"* cries this voice with impatience, *"I'll flatten him so badly that he'll have trouble seeing over the edge of the carpet!"* You have a difficult time keeping this part from storming the gates. Perhaps you can just barely manage to keep it in check. But maybe your inner brute is stronger at this moment. You flip out and batter your enemy with a violent verbal attack. Everyone in the group stares at you in shock – except for one person, Mr Y, who was the target of this hail of bullets. He sits coolly there, flipping idly through his papers. *"If you are quite finished,"* he responds condescendingly, *"could we, perhaps, get on with the work at hand? You said yourself that we are behind schedule."*

The voice of the inner critic

Following this meeting, you have another – with your inner critic. *"What a hopeless loser you are!"* it grumbles inside you. *"You let yourself be trapped by this little upstart, and then you let him provoke you into that kind of an outburst! What do you think that did for your standing in the team? Did you see how they all looked at you? As far as that group is concerned, you're finished! You'd better start looking for a new job. They'll never take you seriously again!"*

With a more aware ego, that wouldn't have happened to you. Let's begin with the last beating, the inner one. You inner critic and your aware "I" exist in a reciprocal relationship. That means that when your aware ego is barely present, let's say, taking up 10 % of the space, your inner critic has 90 %. If you are strongly present as an aware ego in relation to those opposing forces within you, you can stay in touch with them, and you will be able to recognise their intentions. Then you can stand by your actions and decisions without getting attacked later by your inner critic.

You can tell by the reaction of your inner critic how consciously you have acted.

Wait until you see clearly.

What could you do concretely to create more options in such a dilemma? First, don't act immediately; wait and "sweat it out". What does that mean, practically? Perhaps you could ask questions in order to gain some time to let these inner oppositional voices have a say. You turn inward to listen, while on the outside you keep yourself covered. You may find that this inner battle can get rather warm. To cool it down, it is useful to focus your attention on a neutral point, such as your body contact with the chair you are sitting on. When the inner argument has calmed down, you will be clearer about what is important to each of the voices. Now you can intentionally choose a step that will connect the two viewpoints in some meaningful way.

If you want professional support in handling such a situation, coaching may be helpful. The first step is to set up the situation in an individual constellation session with your coach. That will tell you whether there is an issue involved here that goes beyond the situation with Mr Y to touch on company-wide issues. It is possible that you are both representatives, acting out symptoms of the macro-work-system. If that is the case, look for a systemic solution there first. If it is not the case, you can immediately go on to work on your own micro-system. You and your coach look first at the negative relationship pattern that you and Mr Y have fallen into. With the help of the development square, you can see what skills you are missing that Mr Y possesses. Whereas you – or your inner governing body – value yourself as a friendly, understanding, cooperative person, you see Mr Y as arrogant and high-handed.

Next, you ask yourself how Mr Y would describe himself and you. "Arrogant" and "high-handed" would become "self-confident" in his evaluation of himself. Mr Y feels himself to be very important, so he places value on himself. He might describe himself as having a strong ego, in the positive sense. *"Only too right! Too ego-centred!"* says your inner government, but you need to ask for a bit of patience so you can look further. Mr Y would not describe your behaviour as "friendly, understanding and cooperative". He would be more likely to use negative terms such as, "indecisive, wishy-washy, and wimpy", perhaps also "naïve".

Mr Y's behaviour not only pushes all your buttons, it also contains a gift for you. With his unintentional help, you can find a side of yourself that is more self-confident and that has more ego-strength that your inner government has access to.

A conscious evolution has more lasting success than a power break-through.

We would not advise an overthrow of your inner government, as is sometimes tried in power, break-through personality training, as the effects are shortlived. The inner governing body is a coalition that has been formed because of certain necessities. Therefore it is stronger than any of your inner revolutionaries, and you need its support for any durable expansion in your repertoire of behaviour.

Shadow side and light side of Mr Y

"I"	Mr Y.
my light side, which I am identified with: **friendly** **understanding** **cooperative** "This is the way I am!"	shadow side (blind spot) of Mr Y **arrogant** **high-handed** **condescending**
shadow side (blind spot) of 'me' **indecisive** **wishy-washy** **naive**	his light side, which Mr Y is identified with: **self-confident** **self-assured** **rigorous** "This is the way I am!"

Path of development

Openness is not always good.

In the *voice dialogue* process a coach supports you in acknowledging and honouring your inner government. After all, it has done a lot for you. With its consent, you can move towards an inner person who is more self-assured and confident. Now you are standing between two poles that you have previously fought against in external persons. Because you consciously invite both to come into the space of your "I", you gradually become able to be understanding *and* self-confident, cooperative *with* a strong ego at the same time. If you used to approach people at a very personal level, you can now broaden your range to include an "impersonal" option. Being "personal" means always communicating in an open, attentive and warm-hearted way, regardless of who you are dealing with. This "personal" side is reasonable when the other person is also open, without any ulterior motives. For some people, such as Mr Y, openness is not a warm invitation to open up themselves, but a weak spot in another's defences and therefore, a call to attack! The result of such an attack may be that it breaks through to a much less pleasant "personal" side, for example the brute in our case study. It is important for a person who leans towards a "personal" polarity to practice "impersonal" communication. That means using a practical and neutral approach and setting clear boundaries from the start.

194

If your strong point is an "impersonal" communication style, you should experiment with the "personal" variation. Only with both skills will you be in a position to consciously choose and to react appropriately.

With a more aware ego, you have a regulator at your fingertips that functions much like the mixer tap in the shower that allows you to mix warm and cold water until you get the right temperature.

Inner control for external effects

In the next meeting with Mr Y, set your mixer tap a bit cooler, keep your distance, and react to his comments in an impersonal and factual way. It will soon become less interesting for Mr Y to disrupt and provoke if he doesn't succeed with those techniques. He felt flattered and his opinion of you was confirmed as long as you remained helpless and hurt. If he doesn't hit the mark, his egocentric inner governing body will see no advantage in continuing the attack and he will look for a more rewarding target. Your problem is solved; his is not. But that's not your problem.

Good self-management is also good relationship management.

Although the development of an aware ego is neither an ever-lasting solution, nor is it something that happens at mouse-click speed, it helps you concretely in decision-making or conflict situations. In the process of developing ego awareness, you are not looking at the problem, but at the solution. Personality parts that are not coordinated by an inner team leader have only one goal; and that is to push their own viewpoint through. Thus they maintain stubbornly that a task can only be done this way and no other way, even in the face of contradictory information if need be. Their solutions should be taken with a pinch of salt. They are often reminiscent of the man who always bought shoes that were two sizes too small. When asked about this odd choice, he replied, *"To give me pleasure! The most wonderful experience in my whole day is when I take off my shoes in the evening!"*

Power struggles in businesses are often the consequences of inner battles of various personality parts struggling for power. Conflicts with employees or bosses can show us which inner personality parts we have banned from our own repertoire. These parts come at us from the outside in the form of resistance, pressure or harassment.

Resolute focus on a solution that holds the whole working system in view helps in micro-systems just as it does in macro-systems, to find a good order where the needs of the individuals as well as the needs of the whole are taken into consideration. For that we need concrete, practical awareness. This is the organising force of the age of information that helps us to find a better balance in our inner world as well as in our shared "global village". As it is above, so it is below!

6. Beginning to Use Your Systemic Know-How

The methods and processes described in this book are simple and practical and they work, but they are not meant to be a self-help programme. For systemic solutions, you need the help of a qualified consultant or coach who is not a part of your system.

There are however a number of facts that you can look at on your own in terms of their systemic effects. Perhaps in reading this book you have already noticed structures in your company that are systemically favourable or unfavourable. In the following section we have summarised the most important basic principles and problem areas.

If it is clear to you from the following checklist that something in your work system is not in order, you can take appropriate measures. You can correct small deviations yourself without outside help.

For example if a new member of a team is trying to take over and tell the long-standing members how to do things, you don't need a constellation. You know that the principle being violated is of the priority ranking of those who came earlier over those who came later. It should be sufficient to explain this principle to your newcomer person in a private conversation. You can point out that he will fit in better with the team if he takes the last place, and from there asks questions, listens and shares his own knowledge when the others are ready to hear it.

If the scope of the involvement is greater, we recommend that you get support.

The first step is the nearest at hand – the support of your immediate surroundings! Show your colleagues, employees or bosses the following checklist and introduce them to the principles that are favourable to systems. Discuss with your team whether the systemic fundamental orders are correct in your company. Ask about possible violations of basic principles and discuss what a solution might look like. Decide together if you want to do a systemic constellation of the situation.

Professional support

If the answer is yes, proceed only with professional help! Experience has shown that even the best cases of do-it-yourself experiments lead only to more confusion. Go through the questions on the checklist.

The more questions you answer with "no", the clearer the indication of systemic entanglements. If there is interest in clearing it up, a constellation can be helpful.

Systemic checklist

What is, must be allowed to be

- Is the financial situation of the company known to the employees?
- Is the reason for the company (which products/services) explicit and known to everyone?
- Are crises spoken about openly?
- Are mistakes admitted?
- If there have been dismissals or a high employee turnover, are the former employees spoken well of?
- Are performance and success recognised?
- Are customers spoken of with respect in the company?

A Balance of Giving and Taking

- Are the employees committed to the success of the company?
- Do they sometimes work more, or longer when there is a tight spots?
- Do the employees consider their pay reasonable?
- Do they feel recognised by their bosses?
- Are they happy to take responsibility in their areas?
- Is the workload in groups and teams evenly distributed and fair?
- Do management show concern for the needs of their employees?

198

- Do they give clear tasks and instructions?
- Are evaluation meetings experienced as fair by both sides?
- Do the company executives also take personal risks for the firm?
- Do the owners or majority shareholders feel a duty to the company?
- Are the owners or majority shareholders acknowledged and respected by the employees?
- Are profits partially re-invested in the company?
- Are the customers seen and recognised as partners?
- If the relationship between price and performance right for the customers?

The right to belong

- Are the founders of the firm known and recognised?
- Is their history known?
- Do former employees still belong in spirit?
- Are bosses and colleagues talked about with respect in the company?
- Do all employees have the same right to belong?
- Are weaker persons or groups seen as having the same right to belong?
- Do the owners/majority share holders/board directors/top executives feel as if they belong, and do the employees see them as belonging?
- In a crisis, are the employees and management loyal to the company?

Those who came earlier have priority ranking over those who came later

- In companies that are more that twenty years old: Are there traditions? Are they upheld?
- Is long-term involvement honoured (for example, with anniversary celebrations, recognition, or mention in the in-house newspaper?
- Does the experience of long-term employees have a certain status?
- Do the later arrivals in management or amongst employees utilise the experience of those who came earlier?

- Following modernisation or technical innovations, are the old procedures/old products still recognised?
- Do long-term employees/management work constructively and cooperatively when there are innovations, changes and re-structuring?

Priority ranking for higher investment on behalf of the whole, and for competence

- Are the bosses aware of their leadership task regarding the employees?
- Are they taken seriously and respected by the employees?
- Are the decisions of management recognised by the employees?
- Are the company leaders aware of their responsibility for the whole company?
- Do they make visible efforts for the common goals?
- Do they stand by their company and its products in public?
- Are their public statements well received by the employees? Are they seen as believable?
- Do the firm leaders see themselves working in the service of the company and the employees?
- Do the employees speak about the firm, their products and their managers in a positive way?
- Are higher qualifications and competence respected by less competent employees?
- In teams, are the responsibilities of team leaders and team members clearly defined?

Bibliography

Barnett, M. (1991): The Arrow of Man. Zürich (CEC).

Bateson, G. (2002): Mind and Nature: A Necessary Unity. Creskill, NJ (Hampton Press).

Bohm, D. (1980): Wholeness and the Implicate Order. London / Boston (Routledge & Kegan Paul).

Boszormenyi-Nagy, I., G. Spark (1984): Invisible Loyalities. Reciprocity in Intergenerational Family Therapy. Levittown, PA (Brunner / Mazel).

Goleman, D. (1996): Emotional Intelligence. New York (Bantam).

Habermas, J. (1984): The Theory of Communicative Action. Boston (Beacon).

Heidegger, M. (1962): Being and Time. New York (Harper & Row).

Hellinger, B. (2003): To the Heart of the Matter. Heidelberg (Carl-Auer).

Hellinger, B., H. Beaumont, G. Weber (1998): Love's Hidden Symmetry. What Makes Love Work in Relationships. Phoenix, AZ (Zeig & Tucker).

Hellinger, B, G. ten Hoevel (2001): Acknowldeging What is. Phoenix, AZ (Zeig & Tucker).

Husserl, E. (1931): Ideas. New York (Macmillan).

Jantsch, E. (1976): Evolution and Consciousness. Reading, MA (Addison-Wesley).

Laing, R. (1965): The Politics of Experience. London (Tavistock).

Laszlo, E. (1972): Introduction to Systems Philosophy. New York (Gordon Breach).

Maturana, H. R., F. J. Varela (1987): The Tree of Knowledge: The Biological Roots of Human Understanding. Boston (Shambhala).

Pearce, J. C. (1992): Evolution's End. San Francisco (Harper).

Senior, B. (2001): Organisational Change. Harlow (Prentice Hall).

Sheldrake, R. (1981): A New Science of Life. Los Angeles (Tarcher).

Sheldrake, R. (2004): The Sense of Being Stared at: And Other Unexplained Powers of the Human Mind. New York (Arrow).

Stone, H., S. Stone (1987): Embracing Ourselves. San Francisco (New World Library).

Stone, H., S. Stone (1989): Embracing Each Other. Novato, CA (Nataraj).

Stone, H., S. Stone (2000): Partnering. Novato, CA (Nataraj).

Schwartz, R.C. (1995): Internal Family Systems Therapy. New York (Guilford).

Waldrop, M. (1993): Complexity: The Emerging Science at the Edge of Order and Chaos. New York (Touchstone).

Watzlawick, P. (1984): Invented Reality: How Do We Know What We Believe We Know? New York (Norton).

Wilber, K. (1995): Sex, Ecology, Spirituality. Boston (Shambhala).

Index

About the Authors

Klaus P. Horn, born in 1953, is a psychologist as well as a management trainer and consultant. For over twenty years he has served as consultant and management coach for many well-known businesses in Germany and abroad. He is a specialist in the areas of leadership training, systemic coaching, conflict management, team development, and systemic training for trainers.
Contact: info@dr-horn-training.de
www.dr-horn-training.net

Regine Brick, born in 1948, is a psychotherapist and communications trainer as well as a systemic consultant and trainer. She is in private practice and specialises in systemic coaching on professional and personal issues. She also leads an advanced training programme in organisational constellation work and systemic coaching.
Contact: info@dr-horn-training.de
www.dr-horn-training.net

205

Bertold Ulsamer

The Art and Practice of Family Constellations

Leading Family Constellations
as Developed by Bert Hellinger

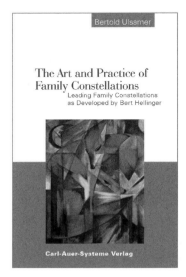

198 Pages, Pb, 2003
ISBN 3-89670-398-6

Using the systemic family therapy developed by Bert Hellinger, tensions and conflicts within families can be revealed. Through the use of representatives, the person involved can observe the psychic dynamics of his or her own family, and identify the patterns which are destructive. In his book, Bertold Ulsamer explains the basis of family constellations, considers the task and the role of the therapist in the field of subjective experience and objective knowledge. He addresses the use of language and the issue of dealing with emotions. His book is aimed at therapists and others who are interested in the practical applications of the Hellinger therapy.

www.carl-auer.com

Fritz B. Simon/Conecta

The Organisation
of Self-Organisation

Foundations of Systemic Management

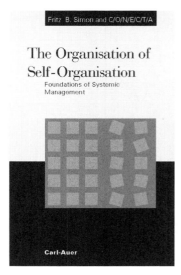

176 Pages, Pb, 2004
ISBN 3-89670-447-8

Economics, so they say, is eighty percent psychology. In this book, the author shows that psychology is one hundred per cent economics. Every human interaction can be understood as a form of market economy. The theoretical explanation for this model follows from recent developments in systems and evolution theory and the epistemological concepts of so-called "radical constructivism".

Human behaviour can be seen as a commodity that is differentiated, named, evaluated and exchanged, and that means that anyone who acts, transacts. This book elucidates what this means in theory and practice for a manager and his everyday life, the organisation of companies, management, achievement, planning and business culture; the author illustrates this in a number of case studies and complements it with recipes for a manager's everyday life.

"A stimulating walk for the inquisitive and the pragmatist over the fairground of our personal behavioural options ... clearly sets this book apart from other management guides on offer." Manager Magazine

Carl-Auer Verlag

Bert Hellinger

To the Heart of the Matter

Brief Therapies

252 Pages, Pb, 2003
ISBN 3-89670-396-X

In his courses and seminars Bert Hellinger works with patients to map out family constellations in a highly concentrated form. This book documents for the first time these highly intensive short-term therapies. These sessions provide insights into the hidden realities and broken relationships revealing new perspectives.

"This book is clearly written, lucid and easy to read. Its profundity will leave a deep impression on the reader."

Systhema

www.carl-auer.com